DISCARD

Adult Diagnostic Reading Inventory

Dr. Pat M. Campbell
and Flo M. Brokop, M.Ed.

*"Meeting the needs of
literacy practitioners and students"*

Grass Roots Press
Edmonton, Alberta

The Adult Diagnostic Reading Inventory is published by
Grass Roots Press

PHONE: 1-780-413-6491
FAX: 1-780-413-6582

EDITING: Judith Tomlinson
COVER DESIGN: Jennifer Windsor
LAYOUT: Barry Boroditsky
PRINTING: Friesens

Canadian Cataloguing in Publication Data

Campbell, Pat, 1958 –
    Adult diagnostic reading inventory

ISBN 1-894593-11-1

    1. Reading (Adult education) – Ability testing. I. Brokop,
Florence, 1958- II. Title.

LC5225.R4C33 2001   428'.0071'5   C2001-900408-7

7th Printing

Printed in Canada

Preface

Welcome to the Adult Diagnostic Reading Inventory (ADRI), an informal reading inventory (IRI) for adults. An IRI is an individually administered diagnostic instrument that allows you to make structured observations of the adult's oral and silent reading performance. Moreover, it enables you to observe how the adult reads in an actual reading situation. The IRI is constructed so that a student can read graded passages at successively higher levels until he/she reaches a point at which he/she can no longer function adequately.

Flo and I have worked in the field of adult literacy and adult basic education since the early 80s. Over the years, we discussed the need for an IRI developed specifically for adult students and educators. The results of these discussions is ADRI, an assessment tool that can be used by adult educators who work with adult students in community-based and college-based settings. We hope students will find the passages both interesting and relevant to their lives.

ADRI is based on the social constructivist theory in which reading is viewed as the active construction of meaning from cues in the text and from the reader's background knowledge within a social context. From this perspective, ADRI is distinguished from many inventories in several ways.

First, the passage topics were chosen by students from across the country, in an effort to recognize the diversity among individuals in terms of race, class, and gender. Second, the student's score is derived from his/her performance on comprehension, in an effort to emphasize the importance of constructing meaning. In other inventories, the student's score is derived from his/her performance in word recognition and comprehension. Finally, the comprehension questions contain a high percentage of inference questions, in an effort to acknowledge the important role of background knowledge in understanding text. In other inventories, the comprehension questions contain only one or two inference questions.

Section One begins with a description of ADRI and ways to use the assessment tool. *Section Two* provides you with information on how to administer and score ADRI. *Section Three* focuses on the interpretation of ADRI. *Section Four* contains the graded word list and the passages for the student. *Section Five* contains the graded word list, passages and comprehension questions for the instructor. Finally, *Section Six* provides you with information on the technical development of ADRI.

Pat Campbell

Acknowledgments

The Adult Diagnostic Reading Inventory (ADRI) was funded by the National Literacy Secretariat, Human Resources Development Canada. The project was sponsored by the Centre for Research on Literacy at the University of Alberta. We appreciate the support and encouragement we received from the national government and the university.

We would like to express our gratitude to the following people who assisted in the development of ADRI by facilitating focus groups, writing passages, fieldtesting the passages, suggesting ideas and/or providing support. A special thank you to Dr. Grace Malicky for guiding us through the development of ADRI.

Pat Campbell and Flo Brokop

Advisory Committee
Audrey Anderson
Gail Douglas
Laurie Gould
Barb Parker
Cate Sills
Jean Smyth

University of Alberta
Dr. Grace Malicky
Dr. Linda Phillips
Centre for Research on Literacy
CRAME Centre for Research
  and Measurement

Writers, Fieldtesters, Facilitators
Sue Arnedt
Norma Baird-Duske
Nancy Bassis
Claudette Bouman
Kevin Bradley
Pat Bragg
Derek Brown
Michelle Brown
Alexandra Campbell
Linda Carnew
Esther Chase
Tomas Clahane
Vicki Cosgrove
Kim Crockatt
Keith Cuyler
Carol Davies
Susan Devins
Jean Edmonson
Betty Gibbs
Vicky Hallett
Carol Hampden
Halynka Honczarenko
Moira Hooten
Parker Israel
Chanmatee Jadoonath
Penny Jensen-Smith
Michael Jodoin
Ann Johnson
Melissa Johnson
Stewart Kallio
Carolyn Kent
Vanessa Kirschner
Linda Kita-Bradley
Bob Kotyk
Lynne Lyon
Paroo Mackinnon
Sherry Mamakwa
Mary McCreadie
Rene Merkel
Gerry Mills
Carol Moore
Linda Moore
Lillian Moore
Lillian Morris
Michelle Noppers
Monika Orzechowska
Meredith Ottoson
Lise Piche-Moor
Cora Reddick
Marg Reine
Jean Reston
Tom Ryan
Irma Sach
Marsha Scribner
Cate Sills
Elise Sheridan
Diane Stenton
Donna Storvik
Jocelyn Stroebel
Cathy Takeda
Jan Thiessen
Vivian Thomas
Lorraine Thornhill
Linda Thorsen
Fred Tibbitt
Johanna Tomkowicz
Don Trembath
Lynn Wallace
Marla White

We would also like to extend our appreciation to the following community colleges and programs, school boards, libraries and literacy programs. The instructors, students and administrators in these settings provided us with the opportunity to fieldtest ADRI.

Fieldtest Sites
Algonquin College
Aurora College
Beacock Library ABE Program
Bedford-Sackville Literacy
  Network
Black Educator's Association
Blossom Park School
Bow Valley College
Cambrian College
Carleton District School Board
College of the North Atlantic
Conestoga College
Crouch Library ABE Program
Dartmouth Literacy Network
Dartmouth Work Activity
  Program
Dryden Literacy Association
Durham Board of Education
Durham College
Elgin County Board of
  Education
Etobicoke School Board
Fanshawe College
Fleming College
G.H. Dawe Library
George Brown College
Georgian College
Haldimand-Norfolk Literacy
  Council
Halifax Regional Library
  Literacy Network
John Howard Society,
  Bowmanville
John Howard Society, Oshawa
Lethbridge Community College
Medicine Hat College
Native Friendship Centre,
  Halifax, NS
New Leaf Literacy
NorQuest College
Nova Scotia Community
  College
NWT Literacy Council
Options Work Activity Program
Oshawa Association for
  Community Living
Portage College
Red Deer College
Red Deer Tutor Bank
Seneca College
Sheridan College
Sudbury Catholic District
  School Board
St. Albert's Adult Learning
  Centre
The Learning Centre Literacy
  Association
Toronto Catholic School Board
Tree of Peace Friendship Centre
Trent University
Trent Valley Literacy Association
Vancouver Community College
Yukon College
YWCA FOCUS program

Table of Contents

Section One

Description of ADRI

ADRI contains a graded word list and passages from Levels 1 to 9, ranging in readability from Grades 1 to 12. Level 1 has four easy and four hard passages. The remaining eight levels each have a selection of four passages, enabling the student to choose a passage of interest and/or familiarity. In order to facilitate pre- and post-testing, the two narrative passages and the two informational passages are parallel in terms of difficulty. At each level there are informational passages on two of the following topics: health, food, sports, animals, personal development, history, and cultures. As well, each level contains narrative passages written in two of the following categories: romance, adventure, true crime and mystery. Finally, each passage is followed by a set of factual and inference questions that reflect an awareness of the two major sources of information students use as they read: background knowledge and text information.

Ways to use ADRI

ADRI can be used for placement or diagnosis. The administration procedures for these two types of testing are described in Section Two. As a placement tool, ADRI will enable you to identify the individual's independent, instructional, and frustration reading levels. Knowledge of an individual's reading levels may be used to determine effective placement in groups, classes, and/or reading material.

When used as a diagnostic tool, ADRI enables you to identify an individual's reading levels. As well, you can analyze the individual's reading errors, retellings, and responses to comprehension questions. You can use knowledge of how the individual processes print (word identification) and text (comprehension) to develop instructional programs.

ADRI includes narrative and informational passages at all levels of reading so that comparisons can be made in how a student reads these different genres. Finally, the graded passages may be used to assess how a student processes print and text. By recording the student's oral miscues, you can learn whether he/she uses meaning, language, and/or print cues to predict words. By asking for a retelling of the passage, you can gain information on how he/she constructs his/her own meaning from the text. Finally, the student's responses to the comprehension questions will provide you with information on his/her use of text information and background knowledge.

Section Two

In this section, you will learn the five steps involved in the administration and scoring of ADRI. You should note that the administration time may take 30 to 60 minutes.

The following suggestions pertain to the administration of ADRI:

✓ Inform the student about who will have access to the test results; e.g., the tutor.

✓ Before you begin administering the test, you should share the purpose and nature of the test with the student.

✓ Reassure the student that this is not a "pass/fail" test; rather, it is a test to see how he/she reads. By understanding the student's strengths and weaknesses, you will be able to provide appropriate instruction.

✓ Ask the student if he/she has any idea about his/her current reading level. Some students have a realistic notion of their reading level, while others do not. At the end of the test, you will need to inform the student of his/her reading level. If the student thought he/she was reading at a Grade 8 level and the testing indicated he/she is reading at a Grade 4 level, you will need to choose your words carefully when you share the test results.

The following five steps are recommended for administering ADRI.

> 1 – Determine the purpose of the assessment.
> 2 – Photocopy Section Five.
> 3 – Determine the entry level.
> 4 – Administer the graded passages.
> 5 – Check the student's comprehension for each passage.

Read on to learn more about these five steps.

1. Determine the purpose of the assessment

Decide whether you want to use ADRI for placement or diagnosis. The administration of the passages (Step 4) depends on the purpose of the assessment.

2. Photocopy Section Five

Instructors must photocopy the word list, passages and questions in Section Five in order to record student responses.

3. Determine entry level

Ask the student to read the graded word list located on page 32.

Begin by saying, "Please look over these columns and choose one you would feel comfortable reading." Once the student has chosen a column, say: "Please read the words out loud. If you do not know a word, you may take a guess. If you want to skip a word, you may."

TIP

Photocopy all of the passages and questions and place them in an expanding desktop file. A desktop file is effective for grouping the passages according to level.

As the student reads the words, record what he/she says. Any word that is pronounced incorrectly should be written as the student pronounced it. Use the following system to record the student's responses as he/she reads the words.

✓	=	correct response
//	=	no response
dk	=	don't know
y-e-s	=	separated letters indicate a naming or sounding out of the letters

TIP
Do an informal check on the student's vocabulary by saying, "Do you know the meaning of all these words?"

After the student reads each list, calculate his/her score. If the student's score is below 90 percent on the first list, drop down to a lower level until he/she achieves 90 percent. Then, ask the student to keep reading more difficult lists until he/she scores 70 percent. At this point, it is time for the student to start reading the passages.

Use the student's performance on the graded word lists to determine an entry level for the reading of the passages. A general rule of thumb is to find the highest word list in which the student has achieved 90 percent word accuracy and to administer the corresponding passage. (If the student scores 90 percent on the Level 1 word list, begin with the Level 1 **easy** passages.)

TIP
If the student can identify only 50 percent or fewer of the words on the Level 1 word list, you should not proceed any further in testing with ADRI.

If the student achieves 100 percent comprehension on the first two passages he/she reads, you can skip a level and move on to a higher level passage. If the student's comprehension score is at frustration level on the first passage he/she reads, have him/her read a passage at a lower level.

Graded Word List

Instructor's Note
The highest level at which the student recognizes 90% of the words in a column should be the starting point for administration of the passages. (If the student scores 90 to 100% at Level 1, the starting point should be the Level 1 easy passages.) Stop when the student misses 3 words in any one column.

1		**2**		**3**	
which	✓	since	✓	neighbor	✓
around	✓	ocean	✓	frightened	✓
mother	mudder	between	✓	exclaimed	✓
something	✓	everyone	✓	chief	✓
thought	✓	friend	✓	farming	frame
children	✓	beautiful	✓	obey	✓
our	✓	kitchen	✓	removed	✓
because	✓	question	✓	serious	✓
every	✓	eight	✓	prepared	✓
could	✓	waited	✓	alarm	✓
	90%		**100%**		**90%**

4		**5**		**6** *entry level -3*	
laughter	ladder	exhausted	✓	fatigue	
impossible	✓	transparent	✓	sympathize	
knowledge	✓	poisonous	dk	accomplishment	
delicious	✓	behavior	✓	yacht	
voyage	✓	merchandise	✓	strenuous	
celebration	✓	considerable	✓	luxurious	
echo	dk	deliberately	✓	occurrence	
hymn	✓	patience	patient	necessity	
nuisance	✓	investigate	✓	alcohol	
guarded	✓	threatened	threat	isolation	
	80%		**70%**		

---

4. Administer the graded passages

The administration of the passages depends on whether you are using ADRI for placement or diagnosis. Administration for the purposes of placement involves having the student silently read each passage and answer the comprehension questions. If you are using ADRI for diagnosis, you will note reading errors (oral miscues) as the student reads the passage out loud. After each passage has been read, you will ask for a retelling before asking the comprehension questions. The following information will describe exactly how to administer ADRI for placement or diagnosis.

ADRI for Placement – Instructions

Every level comprises four passages, with the exception of Level 1. Read the titles and introductions of these passages to the student and ask him/her to select one to read.

Silent Reading

Before the student reads the selection, say,

> *"Here is the passage that you chose to read. Please read it silently to yourself. After you have read the passage, I will ask you some questions."*

Be sure to read the title and introduction of the passage to the student before he/she starts to read the passage.

ADRI for Diagnosis – Instructions

You need to decide whether the student should engage in a prepared oral reading and/or a silent reading. Prepared oral reading is recommended for the student who has difficulty with word identification because this type of administration allows you to record the student's oral miscues or errors. In a prepared oral reading, the student reads the passage twice—the first time silently and the second time orally. Silent reading is appropriate for a student who did not have difficulty identifying the words in the graded word lists.

You may want both to record the student's oral miscues and to obtain a score for silent reading comprehension. In this case, you should have the student engage in prepared oral reading and silent reading at each or some of the levels. For instance, you may ask him/her to read a passage at Level 3 silently, and then have him/her engage in prepared oral reading for a different Level 3 passage.

Every level is comprised of four passages, with the exception of Level 1. Read the titles and introductions of these passages to the student and ask him/her to select one to read.

Silent Reading

Before the student reads the selection, say,

> *"Here is a passage I would like you to read. Please read it silently to yourself. After you have read the passage, tell me about it. Then I will ask you some questions."*

Be sure to read the title and introduction of the passage to the student before he/she starts to read the passage.

TIP

You may wish to tape-record the oral reading. The tape can be used after the assessment to ensure that your recording of oral miscues was accurate. Always be sure to get the student's consent before taping him/her.

Prepared Oral Reading

Before the student reads the selection, say,

> *"Here is a passage I would like you to read. Please read it silently to yourself. When you have finished, please read it out loud to me. While you are reading, I will record the way in which you read. After you have read the passage, tell me about it. Then, I will ask you some questions."*

Be sure to read the title and introduction of the passage to the student before he/she starts to read it.

Record the student's reading errors or oral miscues as he/she reads aloud. (In the interpretation section, you will learn how to analyze the student's oral miscues.) If the student is unable to pronounce a word, wait for five seconds, and then read the word to him/her.

There are six different types of oral miscues that a student can make as he/she identifies words: substitution, pronunciation, omission, addition, inversion, and self-correction. The examples on the following page illustrate how to record the student's oral miscues.

Retelling

Remove the passage from the student's line of vision and ask for a retelling. After you remove the passage, say,

> *"Tell me what you have read, using your own words"* or *"Tell me as much information as you can about what you have just read."*

In the instructor's assessment booklet, each passage is followed by a section titled "Retelling." Write down the student's retelling in the space provided.

Oral Miscues

substitution – One type of substitution occurs when a student says a non-word in place of the text word. Write the substitution above the text word.

colory
A bee colony is made up of three different types of bees.

A substitution also occurs when a student says a word that is different from the printed word. Write the substitution above the text word.

could
Some people caught whitefish.

pronunciation – This occurs when the student does not know the word and you pronounce it for him/her. Provide the word after five seconds, or if the student asks for it.

P
She showed him a ring and a watch.

omission – An omission occurs when the student omits a word, a phrase, a line or part of a word. Circle the omission.

He had on a (winter) hat of some sort and a scarf.

They can get HIV when they share needle(s) with a person who has HIV.

addition – An addition occurs when the student adds a word, a phrase, or part of a word. Indicate the point of addition by a caret and write the added word or words above the text.

was ing
Her heart beat faster as she ran back to the light switch.

inversion – An inversion occurs when the student changes the order of entire words. Draw a curved line for inversions.

After half an hour, she checked outside again.

repetition – A repetition occurs when the student repeats a syllable, a word or a phrase. Draw a line over the repetition.

She went into the pawn shop.

self-correction – A student may spontaneously correct the following oral miscues: substitutions, omissions, additions, and inversions. Place a ✓ after corrected miscues.

crowling ✓
These guys were crawling around the place for two years.

The queen bee is cared (for) by the worker bees.

Self-corrections occur when readers consider what they have said in light of further information. Therefore, this type of oral miscue indicates an ongoing attempt to understand and make sense during reading.

The student's comprehension is the criterion to determine when the student should stop reading the passages.

5. Check the student's comprehension for each passage

Comprehension Questions

If you are using ADRI for placement, ask the questions after the student has read the passage. If you are using ADRI for diagnosis, ask the questions after the retelling, say,

> *"Now I am going to ask you some questions about the passage you have just read."*

Each passage is followed by six to ten comprehension questions. Write down or underline the student's response. In the left-hand column, score the answers as erroneous (0) or correct (1) or partially correct (1/2).

Some questions ask for two or more responses. The student only needs to provide one correct response to receive 1/2 point. For example, if the question asks for four responses and the student provides you with one correct response, he/she should receive 1/2 point. Additional information can be elicited by saying to the student, *"Can you tell me more?"*

Sometimes, a student will find it difficult to answer inference questions because the passage did not contain the answer. You may find that the student's response to an inference question is, "It didn't say.". If this happens, you should provide the student with a prompt by saying, *"This is a 'what do you think' question."*

Reading Level Chart

Immediately determine how many comprehension questions the student answered correctly. Full and half points may be given for responses. Then, refer to the reading level chart, which will tell you whether the student was reading at his/her independent, instructional or frustration level.

Independent	Instructional	Frustration
$7\frac{1}{2}$ – 8 points	$5\frac{1}{2}$ – 7 points	5 points or less

Here is a description of the three levels.

Independent Level

At this level, the student can read fluently. His/her comprehension is excellent and he/she makes very few word recognition errors. The student's recreational reading material and assigned readings should be at the independent level. As well, all homework should be at the independent reading level.

Instructional Level

At this level, the reader has good comprehension and makes some word recognition errors. The student's reading material should be at his/her instructional level when he/she is being taught or tutored.

TIP 5

You may wish to tape-record the retelling. Sometimes a student talks so fast it is easy to miss some of his/her retelling.

Frustration Level
At this level, the student has poor comprehension and may have poor word recognition. The student's rate of reading may be slow and halting. A student should never read material that is at his/her frustration level.

It is not critical to determine the student's independent level. The most important level to obtain is the student's instructional level. The only reason for locating the frustration level is to be sure the student's instructional level has been obtained. If the first passage you administer is at frustration level, be sure to drop down a level and administer easier passages until you have established the instructional level. When the student has reached frustration level, the testing should conclude.

There may be variance between the student's comprehension for narrative and informational passages. So, although he/she may reach frustration level for informational text, he/she may still be able to comprehend narrative text. If you suspect this is the case, you should administer a narrative text at the level at which he/she reached frustration for the information text. For instance, if he/she reached frustration level for informational text at Level 5, you could administer a narrative text at Level 5.

Prior Knowledge

The reading level chart is followed by the question, *"How much did you know about _____ before you read this passage?"* This question focuses on the student's familiarity with the passage. Use this 4-point Likert scale to score this question.

Level of Interest

Finally, ask the student the question, *"How much did you like reading this passage?"* Use this 4-point Likert scale to score the student's response.

LEVEL: 3   READABILITY: Fry – grade 2.5   Dale-Chall – grade 2

Student's Passage page 46

Introduction: This is about the queen bee.

The Queen Bee

heavy

colory

A bee colony is made up of three different types of bees. The biggest bee in a hive

s

is the queen bee. The other bees are called drones and worker bees.

meet

The male bees are the drones. Their purpose in life is to mate with the queen. The

heavy   *sv*

male bees take no part in the work of the hive. The queen bee is cared for by

the worker bees.

also   *fit* *fat*

The queen lays all the eggs in the colony. She only eats and lays eggs. She is fed

data roal jell

a rich diet of royal jelly. The queen lays her eggs from January to November. The

major

majority of eggs are laid between the first warm days of spring and the end of

summer. Sometimes she lays 3,000 eggs per day.

P   *cone*

When an old queen dies, a new queen emerges out of a cocoon. She then stabs

heavy

data

all her sisters to death. There is only one queen bee in a hive.

(158 words)

SECTION FIVE

LEVEL 3

THE QUEEN BEE

RETELLING
Please retell the passage.

The drones do not work. She sometimes lays 3000 eggs per day. The new queen stabs her sisters to death. About how she gets pregnant. The male bee just makes the queen pregnant.

COMPREHENSION

1 (F) Name the three different types of bees.
(queen, worker bee, and drone)

1/2 (F) What is the drone's purpose in life? (to mate with the queen)
to mate

1 (F) What does the queen spend her time doing? Name two things. (eating; mating; laying eggs - 2 out of 3)

1 (I) Which bees do you think have the easiest job and which bees have the hardest job? (drones have the easiest job and worker bees have the hardest job)

0 (F) What does the queen bee eat? (a rich diet of royal jelly)
jell

1 (I) Who do you think feeds the queen royal jelly? (the worker bee)

1 (F) When does the queen lay her eggs? (from January to November; first warm days of spring and the end of summer – 1 out of 2)

1/2 (I) What type of violence occurs in bee colonies? (the new queen stabs all her sisters to death)
she kills her sisters

6/8

READING LEVEL

Independent	Instructional	Frustration
7½ - 8 points	5½ - 7 points	5 points or less

PRIOR KNOWLEDGE
How much did you know about queen bees before you read this passage?

I knew:

1 (nothing) — 2 (very little) — 3 (something) — 4 (a lot)

LEVEL OF INTEREST
How much did you like reading this passage?

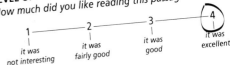

1 (it was not interesting) — 2 (it was fairly good) — 3 (it was good) — 4 (it was excellent)

Section Three

In this section, you will learn how to interpret the student's miscues, retelling, and responses to comprehension questions. Your interpretation of the student's miscues, retelling, and responses to comprehension questions should be based on how the student performed at his/her instructional level. Remember, at the instructional level the student has good comprehension and makes some word recognition errors. Your interpretation should not be based on the student's performance at the frustration level.

At the end of this section, you will find a level 6 passage that illustrates how an examiner analyzed and interpreted a student's miscues and retelling.

Interpreting Word Identification Skills*

If the student engaged in a prepared oral reading, you can begin to analyze and interpret his/her oral miscues. It might take a fair bit of time to analyze your first set of oral miscues, but be patient with yourself. You will gain valuable information that will help you develop the student's instructional program. The more you engage in miscue analysis, the easier it becomes.

A student's oral miscues usually form a pattern. In other words, a student usually repeats the same type of miscue. This pattern reflects how a person reads. By identifying the student's pattern, you can determine the type of instruction he/she needs. There are four common miscue patterns:

- Print-based pattern
- Meaning-based pattern
- Integrative pattern
- Non-integrative pattern

Here you will learn how to analyze each oral miscue that the student made as he/she read the passage. For each uncorrected miscue, decide whether it is print-based (PB), meaning-based (MB), integrative (I) or non-integrative (NI). Then, beside each miscue, print PB, MB, I or N. Once you have completed this analysis, you can determine the student's particular miscue pattern. You can then use this information in planning for instruction.

Print-based

Print-based Miscue — Definition

A print-based miscue does not make sense in relation to the rest of the sentence. Instead, this miscue looks similar to the text word because it contains letters that are in the text word.

Example:

Talk
"Take the ring," she said.

- In this example, the miscue "talk" does not make sense in relation to the sentence.

- The text word "take" and the miscue "talk" look the same. The miscue "talk" contains three of the letters (t, a, k) that are in the text word "take."

---

* The following pages on miscue analysis have been adapted from STAPLE Volume 1 by Pat Campbell and Flo Brokop (Calgary, AB: Literacy Coordinators of Alberta, 1998). STAPLE can be ordered through Grass Roots Press.

Print-based Miscue — Analysis

To determine if a miscue is print-based, ask yourself two questions as you read the sentence:

- Does it look similar to the text word?
- Does it make sense?

If the answer to the first question is yes, and the answer to the second question is no, then it is a print-based miscue.

In order to look similar to the text word, the miscue needs to contain one-half or more of the letters that were in the text word.

In order to make sense, the miscue needs to be meaningful in the sentence. A student may make several miscues in the same sentence. In order to determine if a miscue makes sense, you must read the sentence as the student read it.

Print-based Miscue Pattern — Definition

A print-based miscue pattern occurs when the majority of the student's miscues are print-based.

Example:

        verse   *salmon*

HIV is a virus. It is found in blood. It is found in semen. It is found in

vagal flowed

vaginal fluid. There are two ways men and women can get HIV.

They can get HIV when they have sex with a person who has HIV.

                          shore

They can get HIV when they share needles with a person who has HIV.

- In this example, the majority of the miscues do not make sense in relation to the sentence.

- The majority of the text words and miscues look similar. For example, the miscue "shore" contains four of the letters (s, h, r, e) that are in the text word "share."

- Miscues that are non-words are indicative of a person with a print-based pattern. For example, the miscue "vagal" is a non-word.

Print-based Miscue Pattern — Planning for Instruction

When the majority of miscues are print-based, the students are paying a lot of attention to letters and sounds. These students need to pay more attention to meaning and will need to learn to use context clues to predict unfamiliar words. They will need to make more effective use of their background knowledge when they read. These readers would benefit from instruction in the cloze procedure*.

---

* See Glossary, p. 185

Meaning-based

Meaning-based Miscue — Definition

A meaning-based miscue is defined as one that makes sense in the sentence but does not look like the text word. Although it does make sense in the sentence, it might change the author's intended meaning.

Example:

lady
Then the man gave the woman a ticket.

- In this example, the miscue "lady" makes sense in relation to the sentence.

- The text word "woman" and the miscue "lady" do not look the same. The only letter they have in common is the letter "a."

Example:

street
I saw that guy as I left your place.

- In this example, the miscue "street" is a meaning-based miscue because it makes sense in the sentence, even though it changes the author's intended meaning.

Meaning-based Miscue — Analysis

To determine if a miscue is meaning-based, ask yourself two questions as you read the sentence:

- Does it look similar to the text word?

- Does it make sense?

If the answer to the first question is no and the answer to the second question is yes, then it is a meaning-based miscue.

In order to make sense, the miscue needs to make sense within the sentence. You need to read all the student's miscues in a sentence in order to determine if a single miscue makes sense within the sentence.

For omissions and additions, you need only ask, *"Does it make sense?"* If the answer is yes, then it is a meaning-based miscue.

Meaning-based Miscue Pattern — Definition

A meaning-based pattern occurs when the majority of the student's miscues are meaning-based. Quite often, a meaning-based pattern contains a lot of omissions and additions simply because the reader is not paying attention to the print.

Example:

a river
Métis people lived near the lake. The lake had pike, perch, and
Many
jackfish. Métis people ate lots of fish as well as meat. Some people
their
caught whitefish. People fished with nets. They fished all year round.

In winter they ice fished.

- In this example, the miscues make sense in relation to the sentence.
- There are one addition and two omissions, indicating that the reader was not always paying attention to print.
- The miscues ("river" for "lake" and "many" for "Métis") do not look similar to the text word.

Meaning-based Miscue Pattern — Planning for Instruction

When the majority of miscues are meaning-based, it means that the students rely too heavily on meaning context and their background knowledge to predict unfamiliar words. This sometimes results in a situation where the students' meaning is quite different from that intended by the author. These students need to pay more attention to print (letters, sounds, word parts) to figure out unfamiliar words, while continuing to think about the meaning. They would benefit from work on word families, word sorts, and word blitzing*.

Integrative

Integrative Miscue — Definition

An integrative miscue occurs when the miscue makes sense in the sentence and is visually similar to the text word.

Example:

case

They can learn about the causes of HIV.

- The miscue "case" makes sense in relation to the sentence.
- The text word "causes" and the miscue "case" look the same. The miscue "case" contains 4 letters (c, a, s, e) that are in the text word "causes."

Integrative Miscue — Analysis

To determine if a miscue is integrative, ask yourself two questions as you read the sentence:

- Does it look similar to the text word?
- Does it make sense?

If the answer to both questions is yes, then it is an integrative miscue.

Integrative Miscue Pattern — Definition

A pattern of integrative miscues occurs when many of the miscues are integrative and/or there is a balance of meaning-based and print-based miscues. At least some miscues in an integrative pattern will be self-corrected. Corrected miscues indicate that the reader is monitoring his/her comprehension.

---

* See Glossary, p. 205

Example:

       olden   *assist*

In old times a farm woman had to work hard. She often assisted her

          on   *farm*   *cotton*

husband in the fields. She looked after chickens and cattle. A farm

         provided   *which* ✓

woman preserved food to eat in winter.

                                   Dirt

It was difficult to keep the house clean. Dust and mud came into the

  home

house because there were no sidewalks outside. Someone had to

sweep and scrub the floor(s.)

- In this example, the majority of the miscues ("olden" for "old", "provided" for "preserved") are integrative because they make sense in relation to the sentence and look the same as the text word.

- In one instance, the reader self-corrected a miscue ("which" for "winter") that did not make sense.

Integrative Miscue Pattern — Planning for Instruction
When the pattern of miscues is integrative, it means that the student uses a combination of print, context clues, and background knowledge to predict unfamiliar words. Once the word is predicted, the student confirms his/her prediction by seeing if it makes sense in the rest of the sentence or passage. If the word does not make sense, the student might make a second attempt at predicting the word.

This type of reader possesses a variety of strategies for decoding unfamiliar words. This is the pattern of a good reader.

Non-integrative

Non-integrative Miscue — Definition
A non-integrative miscue occurs when the miscue is not meaningful and does not look like the text word. Also, a word that you pronounced for the student is classified as a non-integrative miscue.

Example:

                    P

They have a big brain for their size.

- The tutor pronounced this word for the student. He/she was unable to use background knowledge or print to figure out the word "brain." Therefore, the miscue is non-integrative.

Example:

         p-e-

The lake had pike, perch, and jackfish.

- The student attempted to sound out the text word "pike." However, the miscue "p-e-" neither looks like the text word nor does it make sense.

Example:

man

Wild rice is a tall grass-like plant.

- The miscue "man" does not make sense, nor does it look like the text word "grass."

Non-integrative Miscue — Analysis
To determine if a miscue is non-integrative, ask yourself two questions as you read the sentence:

- Does it look similar to the text word?

- Does it make sense?

If the answer to both questions is no, then it is a non-integrative miscue. As well, words that you pronounce for the student are classified as non-integrative miscues.

Non-integrative Miscue Pattern — Definition
A non-integrative miscue pattern occurs when most of the miscues do not make sense and do not look similar to the text word. A person with this type of pattern often waits for you to pronounce unfamiliar words. As well, he/she has a rate of reading that is painstakingly slow. This type of pattern occurs primarily among students who are very beginning readers.

Example:

Are   S-m-   P   P
Ants are smart. They have a big brain for their size. Ants can smell
     This   make   own
food. They can smell a mate. They speak to each other with their

smell. They ask each other for help.

- In this example, the majority of the miscues are non-integrative. There are two instances ("are" for "ants" and "own" for "other") where the student did not use background knowledge or print to figure out the unfamiliar word.

- The student relied on the tutor to pronounce two of the words.

Non-integrative Miscue Pattern — Planning for Instruction
This type of reader needs to use a combination of print and background knowledge to predict words when he/she reads. This type of reader has not learned how to use print and background knowledge effectively when he/she reads. This reader needs to be taught a variety of word recognition strategies. These strategies include word families, cloze*, and phonics.

---

* See Glossary, p. 205

Interpreting Comprehension Skills

Many readers have well-developed word recognition skills, yet they still have difficulty comprehending written material. If the student has difficulty comprehending text, you will need to understand how the student interacts with text in order to develop an effective instructional program. In this section, you will learn how to analyze the student's responses to comprehension questions and his/her retelling.

Questions to Guide Interpretation

The student's responses to questions can add to your understanding of his/her comprehension by allowing you to see whether the student integrates information from the text with his/her background knowledge. Here are two questions to ask yourself as you analyze his/her responses to comprehension questions:

- What percentage of inference questions are answered correctly?

If the student is able to answer 70 percent of the inference questions correctly on instructional level material, he/she is able to adequately integrate text-based and knowledge-based information to draw inferences from what he/she has read.

- What percentage of factual questions are answered correctly?

If the student is able to answer 70 percent of the factual questions correctly on instructional level material, he/she is able to adequately process text information in this material.

The retelling can add to your understanding of a student's comprehension by allowing you to get a view of the quantity, quality and organization of information gleaned during reading. This information has implications for instruction. Here are three questions to ask yourself as you analyze the retelling:

- What was the student's interest in and familiarity with the passage?

If the student did not possess any background knowledge, or experience about or interest in the topic, he/she may have difficulty comprehending the passage. Consequently, the retelling might be brief. As well, the retelling may contain a limited amount of inferential information and quite a bit of erroneous information.

- Do the retellings of informational passages retain their basic structure?

The retelling should be organized around the main idea and supporting details. This type of retelling suggests the student has internalized the structure of informational passages. If the main idea and/or supporting details are not included in the retelling, the student may require some instruction in the structure of informational passages.

- Do the retellings of narrative passages retain the basic structure of the narratives?

The retelling should contain information related to all four categories of story structure: setting/background, goal, events, and resolution. As well, the retelling should follow the appropriate sequence of the story. This type of retelling suggests that the student has internalized the structure of the story and is able to use it in his/her recall. If the four categories are not reflected in the retelling, the student may require some instruction in story structure.

The Student's Retelling

Although there is no way to directly observe the comprehension process, the analysis of the student's retelling does provide insight into the reader's comprehension processes. To analyze the retelling, follow these steps:

1. Divide the retelling into idea units using slashes. An idea unit is usually a simple sentence; compound or complex sentence is two idea units.

2. Compare each idea unit to the passage that was read by the student.

3. Code each idea unit. There are five categories for coding idea units: explicit, synthesis, inference, elaboration, and erroneous. Refer to the chart for a definition of each category and an example.

Explicit

The idea unit contains specific references from one or more sentences within the passage. Some of the information in the idea unit may have been changed. For example, the student may say "they" when the text word was "people" or "house was burning" for the "house was on fire."

TEXT: I saw an old man get on the bus.

IDEA UNIT: **An old man got on the bus.**

TEXT: Linda has a part-time job at the diner. She works in the morning from six until ten.

IDEA UNIT: **Linda works in the diner till ten.**

Synthesis

A synthesis is similar to a generalization or main idea statement from one or more sentences in the passage.

TEXT: Steve looked under the truck. He saw what was wrong. A rock was attached to the drive shaft with wire. Steve then knew it was just a grad trick. His friends Neil and Shawn were laughing out of control behind a nearby bush.

IDEA UNIT: **Some of his buddies played a practical joke on him.**

Inference

An inference occurs when the reader is "reading between the lines" or filling in the gaps in the text. An inference always has a connection to the information in the text. You should be able to refer to the text and find information that led to the inference.

TEXT: Ramadan is one month long. It is a special time for Muslims. They pray and fast each day.

IDEA UNIT: **Ramadan is very sacred.**

Elaboration

An elaboration is triggered by information in the text. It is different from an inference in that it has no connection to the text. Instead, an elaboration is based personal experiences. In other words, two students would probably not make the same elaboration.

TEXT: Also, make a mental list of the standard prices of your usual purchases. By doing this, you will know a bargain when you see one. Finally, use coupons only for the items on your list. You aren't saving money if you use the coupons on foods you don't need in the first place.

IDEA UNIT: **And you can buy cheaper stuff at different stores than other stores.**

Erroneous

The category includes specific errors in such areas as dates, proper nouns, substitutions, etc. The errors might be due to memory or lack of attention to the text. Sometimes, the student makes conceptual errors. For instance, the passage says "They were detained in internment camps" and the student says "They were prisoners of war."

TEXT: I saw an old man get on the bus.

IDEA UNIT: **An old man got on the train.**

Your analysis of the student's responses to comprehension questions and to the retelling will help you to determine the student's comprehension pattern. A student's understanding of text depends on how he/she interacts with text. The student's responses to comprehension questions and his/her retelling usually form a pattern. There are three common comprehension patterns:

- Text-based pattern
- Knowledge-based pattern
- Integrative pattern

Read on to learn how to identify these patterns.

> When we talk about miscue patterns, we use the word "print-based", but when we talk about comprehension patterns, we use the word "text-based."

Text-based

Text-based Comprehension Pattern — Definition

Learners with a text-based comprehension pattern are usually able to answer the factual comprehension questions. The answers to these types of questions are in the text or passage. However, these students often have difficulty answering inference questions, where they have to use background knowledge to "read between the lines."

> Each comprehension question is coded **F** for factual or **I** for inference.

The majority of information in their retelling is explicit information. The retelling does not usually contain inferences or elaborations.

Example:

TEXT: She went into the pawn shop. She said, "I need some money." He said, "What can you sell?" She showed him a ring and a watch.

"Take the ring," she said. "Are you sure?" He asked. "Yes. Take it." The man took the ring. He put it in a box.

Then the man gave the woman some money. He gave her $120. The woman took the money. Then the man gave the woman a ticket. The woman took the ticket. She began to cry.

RETELLING:

Explicit   Explicit

She need some money/and she went to a pawn

shop to pawn a ring and a watch/and the man

Explicit   Explicit

asked her if she was sure./ She said yes. / The

Explicit   Explicit

man took the ring/and he gave her $120 with

the ticket.

Text-based Comprehension Pattern — Analysis

To determine if a comprehension pattern is text-based, ask yourself these questions:

- Is the student able to correctly answer factual questions?

- Does the student have difficulty answering inference questions?

- Does the retelling contain a great deal of explicit information?

- Does the retelling contain few inferences and elaborations?

If the answers to these questions is yes, the student probably has a text-based comprehension pattern.

Text-based Comprehension Pattern — Planning for Instruction

Students with a text-based comprehension pattern need to rely more on their background knowledge when they read. Students need to relate their background knowledge with the text information. Before these students begin to read something, they should read the title and try to predict what it might be about. As they are reading, the students should continually relate what they are reading to what they know.

Knowledge-based

Knowledge-based Comprehension Pattern — Definition

Students with a knowledge-based comprehension pattern use their background knowledge, rather than information from the text, to answer comprehension questions. They often have difficulty answering factual questions. Sometimes, the students use their background knowledge to answer factual questions.

The majority of information in their retelling is inferences or elaborations. Although it is appropriate to use background knowledge, an over-reliance on prior knowledge can lead to problems because the reader's understanding of the passage may differ from the author's intended meaning.

Example:

TEXT: Joe saw an ad in the paper. It said, "Pianos for Sale - $199."

"What a deal" thought Joe. "I can buy a piano for $199. I can sell it for ten times as much! This is too good to be true!" Joe sent the piano company a check.

Six weeks later, Joe got a small box in the mail. He opened the box. Inside, was a little plastic piano.

Joe got mad. He phoned the Better Business Bureau. The man on the phone asked Joe for the name and address of the piano company. The address was only a postbox number.

RETELLING: *Inference*
Joe got too excited by seeing the price of the
Elaboration
piano and/ he shouldn't have mailed them money/
Elaboration   *Explicit*
but you just don't do that/it was a post box
Inference
number/ so he got stung with the plastic piano.

Knowledge-based Comprehension Pattern — Analysis
To determine if a comprehension pattern is knowledge-based, ask yourself these questions:

- Is the student able to correctly answer inference questions?

- Does the student have difficulty answering factual questions?

- Does the retelling contain a great deal of inference and elaborations, rather than explicit information?

If the answer to these questions is yes, the student probably has a knowledge-based comprehension pattern.

Knowledge-based Comprehension Pattern — Planning for Instruction
Students with a knowledge-based comprehension pattern need to rely more on the text information when they read. When they are reading narrative passages, they need to pay more attention to the characters (who), the setting (where, when), the plot (what, why). When they are reading informational passages, they need to pay more attention to the main ideas and details.

Integrative

Integrative Comprehension Pattern — Definition
Students with an integrative comprehension pattern use their knowledge and text information to answer comprehension questions. This type of reader is able to answer factual and inference questions.

The information in their retelling comes from their background knowledge and from the text. Therefore, the retelling contains explicit information, inferences, and elaborations. As well, the retelling contains synthesis statements that combine information from the text.

Example:

TEXT: **The One-Room School House**
There was a stove in the school. The stove burned wood and coal. Wet mitts hung near the stove. The room smelled like wet wool.

The teacher had a desk at the front. The children had desks in rows. The little children sat together. The big boys sat at the back. Sometimes they got into trouble.

The teacher wrote on the blackboard. The children wrote down the lesson. At recess the children played outside. They build snow forts. They threw snowballs. Then they hung their mitts by the stove again.

RETELLING:

        Synthesis   Elaboration
It's about an old school house/ really, really old/
   Inference   Explicit
has no electricity/has only one room/teacher is
  Explicit
up by the blackboard and writing down every-
           Explicit   Inference
thing/they have a stove/that heats the place/
          Explicit
and then when they went out for recess/they
       Inference
wet their mittens playing in the snow

Integrative Comprehension Pattern — Analysis

To determine if a comprehension pattern is integrative, ask yourself these questions:

- Is the student able to correctly answer both factual and inference questions?

- Does the retelling contain a combination of explicit information, inferences, elaborations and synthesis statements?

If the answer to these questions is yes, the student probably has an integrative comprehension pattern.

Integrative Comprehension Pattern — Planning for Instruction

Students with an integrative comprehension pattern use a combination of background knowledge and text information in an effort to understand the author's message. This type of reader is actively involved with the text. For instance, he/she uses his/her background knowledge to make predictions and inferences. As well, he/she understands the importance of paying attention to the author's message. This is the pattern of a good reader.

---

* The following pages on miscue analysis have been adapted from STAPLE Volume 1 by Pat Campbell and Flo Brokop (Calgary, AB: Literacy Coordinators of Alberta, 1998). STAPLE can be ordered through Grass Roots Press.

Example:
The following Level 6 passage illustrates how to analyze a student's miscues and retelling.

This passage was read by a 25 year old male student whose mother tongue was English. The test results indicate that the student's instructional level is Level 6. This means that his reading materials should have a readability level that ranges between grades 5 to 6.

The student has well developed comprehension skills. He was able to answer both factual and inference questions. An analysis of his retelling indicates an integrative comprehension pattern.

An analysis of the student's miscues indicates that he has a print-based word identification pattern. The majority of his miscues are visually similar to the text word, but do not make sense. He needs to pay more attention to meaning and will need to learn to use context clues to predict unfamiliar words. He would benefit from instruction in the cloze procedure and in decoding multisyllabic words. He corrected 1/3 of his miscues, which indicates that he sometimes monitors for meaning.

LEVEL: 6

READABILITY: Fry – grade 5.5   Dale-Chall – grade 5-6

Student's Booklet: page 34
Introduction: This is the story of a woman's yearly visit to a special hotel.

print-based word identification pattern

Greta's Vigil

Greta paid for the hotel room. She carried her luggage to the second floor corner

room, just as she had done for 28 years. The room was a bit more expensive now.

quantity PB

Each year, the price went up a little, and the quality of the hotel lessened. But

she expected that. The years had not been kind to her either.

When she was a bride those many years ago, her groom had gently lifted her

threadhole PB   suit PB

and carried her over the threshold of Number 3 suite. Greta closed her eyes and

hugged her body, recalling how her arms and his fit perfectly around each other,

brace PB

and how much the couple was in love. How she longed now to feel his embrace.

There was a wonderful scent about Philip, she recalled. Was she dreaming, or

_____ way ✓

did she smell that sweet odor right now?

sharlit PB

That bright, starlit night in May lived in Greta's memory as clearly as if it had

been just yesterday. Many gray hairs and unwanted wrinkles had appeared since

then. She hoped Philip would still find her attractive. From her suitcase, she produced

a framed snapshot of a smiling wedding couple. Yes, she had changed quite a lot

tatred PB

the I

since that photo was taken. She laid out her lacy nightgown on the tattered bedspread.

She carefully placed a red rose upon the pillow as she turned back the covers.

Greta heard her lover say, "We need champagne! I'll be right back, darling.

This is (to be ✓) a special evening. By the way, did I mention I love you more than

bursh PB

(life ✓) itself?" She felt a gentle kiss brush her lips, and he was gone – just as it had

been 28 years ago.

went ✓

Greta waited for his return, as she did on each anniversary of her wedding and

of her husband's death. (300 words)

LEVEL 6

GRETA'S VIGIL

RETELLING
Please retell the story.

Explicit   Synthesis
Her husband passed away/so every anniversary she would rent a
                                                    Inference
hotel and still celebrate it/she would think he was still with her/

Inference
and hopefully he would come back

Integrative comprehension pattern

COMPREHENSION

__1__ (F) What was Greta waiting for? *(the return of her husband)*

__1/2__ (F) Name two ways the hotel had changed since Greta's first stay. *(the hotel prices had gone up a little, and the quality of the hotel had been lowered)*

hotel prices had gone up a little

__1__ (I) How many times a year did Greta return to the hotel? *(once a year)*

__1__ (F) What did Greta remember about their last night together? Name four things. *(being carried over the threshold; how their arms fit perfectly around each other; how much they were in love; Philip's scent; Philip's gentle kiss; Philip's last words; that he went to get champagne – 4 out of 9)*

__0__ (I) During what season did Greta and Philip marry? *(spring, ask "what season" if the student says "May")*

I don't know

__1__ (I) How old do you think Greta is? *(any answer that indicates that she is in her late 40s or older is acceptable)*

__1__ (F) Name three things that Greta brought with her to the hotel room. *(rose; wedding photo; lacy nightgown; suitcase – 3 out of 4)*

__1__ (I) On what night did Philip die? *(on his honeymoon; on his wedding night; a night in May – 1 out of 3)*

__0__ (F) Before his death, what did Philip want to buy? *(champagne)*

a house

__1__ (I) How many years had Greta been a widow? *(28 years)*

READING LEVEL

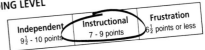

Independent 9½ - 10 points	Instructional 7 - 9 points	Frustration 6½ points or less

LEVEL OF INTEREST
How much did you like reading this story?

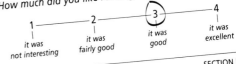

1	2	3	4
it was not interesting	it was fairly good	it was good	it was excellent

SECTION FIVE

149

Section Four

Word List

A	B	C
which	since	neighbor
around	ocean	frightened
mother	between	exclaimed
something	everyone	chief
thought	friend	farming
children	beautiful	obey
our	kitchen	removed
because	question	serious
every	eight	prepared
could	waited	alarm

D	E	F
laughter	exhausted	fatigue
impossible	transparent	sympathize
knowledge	poisonous	accomplishment
delicious	behavior	yacht
voyage	merchandise	strenuous
celebration	considerable	luxurious
echo	deliberately	occurrence
hymn	patience	necessity
nuisance	investigate	alcohol
guarded	threatened	isolation

Word List

G

testimonial

synthetic

maneuver

pneumonia

poise

immune

lyric

prohibited

siesta

hysterical

H

persuasive

capillary

commemorate

conscientious

jostle

susceptible

inquisitive

pretentious

affiliated

rendezvous

I

conscription

recipient

domicile

diminutive

euphoria

exonerate

nausea

fictitious

transactions

nuptial

Cats

Some people have cats. Cats like to sleep. They can sleep all day. They like to sleep in the sun. Cats do not like to get wet. Cats like to eat meat. They like to drink milk. Cats are good pets.

Mary and her Son

Mary is mad. Her son is late. He is 14. He is out with his friends. Her son gets home at two. Mary gets mad at her son. Then her son gets mad. He says he is not a kid.

Joe Gets a Dog

Joe is sad. He is 68. He lives alone. He does not like to live alone. His friend says get a dog. Joe gets a dog. Joe says his dog is his best friend.

Sam and Pat

Sam went to the store. He had to get milk. He met Pat at the store. Pat had to get dog food. Sam liked Pat. He asked Pat out on a date. She said yes. Sam was very happy.

Losing Body Fat

It takes time to lose body fat. The key is to exercise and eat right. You need to exercise at least three times a week. Ride a bike. Go for a jog. Go for a swim. Walk the dog. Run up and down the stairs.

You should change the way you shop and eat. Look for fat-free foods in the store. Do not eat candy and chips. Eat lots of fish, grains, and fruit. Soon, you will begin to look slim and trim.

Ants

Most ants build their nests in soil and sand. Three kinds of ants live in the nest. The male ant mates with the queen. The queen ant lays the eggs. The worker ants have many jobs.

They watch the nest. They can bite and sting. The worker ants will fight until they die. An ant fight can last up to 16 hours. The worker ants hunt for food. They bring the food back to the nest. They also keep the nest clean.

The End

She went into the pawn shop. She said, "I need some money." He said, "What can you sell?" She showed him a ring and a watch.

"Take the ring," she said. "Are you sure?" he asked. "Yes. Take it." The man took the ring. He put it in a box.

Then the man gave the woman some money. He gave her $120. The woman took the money. Then the man gave the woman a ticket. The woman took the ticket. She began to cry.

Ted and the Cop

The cop said, "Did you do it?" Ted just looked at him. Then the cop said, "Where did you dump the body?" Ted just kept looking at him.

"We know you did it," said the cop. "Your friend told us." Ted just looked at the cop. Ted thought, "Dumb cop. Cops are so dumb."

Then the cop turned off the tape recorder. "Get out!" he yelled. "Get out of here!" Ted laughed at the cop. He laughed because he knew he would get away with it.

AIDS

HIV is a virus. It is found in blood. It is found in semen. It is found in fluid from the vagina.

There are two ways men and women can get HIV. They can get HIV when they have sex with a person who has HIV. They can get HIV when they share needles with a person who has HIV.

At first, people with HIV feel fine. After a few years, people with HIV can start to get sick. HIV can turn into AIDS after two to ten years. When they have AIDS, their bodies cannot fight other diseases. Many people with AIDS have died.

There is no cure for AIDS. But people can prevent HIV. They can learn about the causes of HIV. Also, people can protect themselves. They can practice safe sex by using condoms. They can use clean needles.

The Polar Bear

Polar bears get most of their food from the ocean. Polar bears have a layer of blubber. It keeps them warm when they swim. The tiny webs between their toes help them swim.

The polar bear's coat is white. This colour makes it difficult for them to be seen on snow and ice. These bears have two layers of fur. The inner layer of fur is thick. This makes it hard for water to get to the skin. There is oil in their hair and skin. The oil helps to make them waterproof. They are the only bears with hair on the bottom of their feet. This hair keeps their feet warm. It keeps them from slipping on ice and snow.

Bad Food

Ron and Donna are husband and wife. Ron is a very big man. He is strong. Donna is a small woman. She is a nurse.

One day Ron and Donna went out for dinner. Donna had a salad. Ron ate fish and chips. Then they went to the zoo.

Ron got sick. His legs and arms were weak. He could not walk because of the pain in his stomach. He was very hot. Then he was too cold. Donna knew Ron had eaten some bad fish. She helped him to the car.

They drove to the hospital. The doctor said Ron had food poisoning. She gave Ron some pills to make him better.

Rock and Roll

It was grad night. Steve was all dressed up for the dance. He was in a hurry. He jumped into his truck. Steve knew he was running late. As his truck pulled away from the curb, he heard a noise from below it. He was driving at a slow speed. His truck was rocking and rolling like a ride at the fair.

Steve stopped the truck. He swore under his breath. In his fancy suit, he got down on his knees. Steve looked under his truck. He saw what was wrong. A rock was attached to the drive shaft with wire. Steve then knew it was just a grad trick. His friends Neil and Shawn were laughing out of control behind a nearby bush.

The Queen Bee

A bee colony is made up of three different types of bees. The biggest bee in a hive is the queen bee. The other bees are called drones and worker bees.

The male bees are the drones. Their purpose in life is to mate with the queen. The male bees take no part in the work of the hive. The queen bee is cared for by the worker bees.

The queen lays all the eggs in the colony. She only eats and lays eggs. She is fed a rich diet of royal jelly. The queen lays her eggs from January to November. The majority of eggs are laid between the first warm days of spring and the end of summer. Sometimes she lays 3,000 eggs per day.

When an old queen dies, a new queen emerges out of a cocoon. She then stabs all her sisters to death. There is only one queen bee in a hive.

A Pioneer Woman

In old times a farm woman had to work hard. She often assisted her husband in the fields. She grew a vegetable garden for food. She looked after chickens and cattle. Or she made the children look after them.

A farm woman preserved food to eat in winter. She preserved meat and fish with salt. She dried berries and other foods. Every day she cooked the family meals.

It was difficult to keep the house clean. Dust and mud came into the house because there were no sidewalks outside. There were no vacuum cleaners. Someone had to sweep and scrub the floors.

If children were sick, the mother would nurse them. There were few doctors or hospitals in the country.

It was a lonely life for a woman. Most farms were far away from neighbors. The men were away working or hunting a lot of the time.

Summer Romance

Ann and Mike were students. They met one summer in an English class. Ann was from Spain. Mike was from Poland. They spent a lot of time with each other and fell in love. When the summer ended, Ann had to go back to Spain, and Mike had to go back to Poland. Before they parted, Mike promised to visit Ann in Spain.

Mike wrote to Ann every week. At first, Ann answered all his letters. Then Mike began to get fewer letters from Ann, but each letter from her was still full of love.

The next summer, Mike went to visit Ann in Spain. When he got there, he phoned her from the airport. Ann's sister answered the phone. She told Mike that Ann was married. Mike went back to Poland. He wrote Ann his last letter. It said: "You knew I was coming to visit. Why didn't you tell me you were married? I thought you loved me. I guess, for you, it was just a summer romance."

The Piano Lesson

Joe saw an ad in the paper. It said, "Pianos for Sale – $199."

"What a deal!" thought Joe. "I can buy a piano for $199. I can sell it for ten times as much! This is too good to be true!" Joe sent the piano company a check.

Six weeks later, Joe got a small box in the mail. He opened the box. Inside, was a little plastic piano.

Joe got mad. He phoned the Better Business Bureau. The man on the phone asked Joe for the name and address of the piano company. The address was only a postbox number. The man checked his records. He told Joe that there was no record of the piano company.

Joe was sad. He had lost a lot of money on a little piano. But he did learn a big lesson – some things *are* too good to be true.

Hay Fever

In the United States, about one in ten people suffers from hay fever. This condition causes sneezing, wheezing, and runny noses. It also makes the eyes red and swollen. The ears, nose, eyes, mouth, and skin may get itchy. Hay fever is often confused with the common cold.

Hay fever is an allergy to pollen. Some people are sensitive to tree pollen and snow mold. For these people, hay fever is worse in the spring. Others are sensitive to grass pollen. For these people, hay fever is worse during the summer. Some people suffer all year long. This is because they are allergic to dust mites and animal hair. Yeast, eggs, and milk have also been known to trigger hay fever.

There is no cure for hay fever. But, there are ways to control it. People should avoid pollens, molds, dust, and animals. Windows should be closed when pollen is in the air. People should also avoid going outdoors on hot, dry, windy days. They should spend time outside during the evening, rather than the day. This is when the pollen count is the lowest. To avoid dust, mattresses, box springs, and pillows should be cleaned. Then they should be covered with dust-proof covers.

There are a few ways to treat hay fever. People can buy tablets, nasal sprays, and eye drops. Some of these drugs need to be prescribed by a doctor. Others can be purchased over the counter. Finally, people can get allergy shots before hay fever season begins.

Beaver Lodges

The beaver is the largest rodent in the United States. Beavers live in lodges located in lakes, rivers, ponds, and streams. Sometimes they construct dams in ponds and streams. The dams maintain a water supply to protect their lodges.

Beavers use their sharp teeth to gnaw through the trunks of young trees. Often, a newly felled tree will be a long way from the beaver's dam or lodge. If this happens, the beaver floats the log to the building site. Sometimes, it builds canals to let the log float freely. The beaver uses its front paws to put the trunks and branches into place.

The walls of the lodge are layers of logs held together with grass, debris, and mud. The roof, made of branches, is about three feet above the water level. A chimney is built into the roof to let air flow in and out of the lodge.

The entrance to the lodge is under water. The living room is above the water level. A tunnel connects the entrance to the living room. There is more than one exit from the lodge. This helps the beaver to escape if an enemy tries to enter.

Sometimes, many families live together in a colony. Each family builds and lives in its own lodge. An adult pair, newborn kits, and yearlings born the previous year occupy each lodge. Beavers spend most of their day building or fixing their lodge and dam.

The Unlucky Bank Robber

A heavyset man entered a bank and sat down in a chair in the reception area. He picked up a magazine and pretended to read it. After a couple of minutes, he lowered the magazine and surveyed his surroundings. He observed the security guards, noting that there were two of them and they both had guns. His gaze turned towards the bank tellers behind the shiny, protective glass. Then, he happened to glance up at the vaulted ceiling. He saw a skylight – and smiled. He put down the magazine and went home.

The man waited for the sun to set, and then he returned to the bank. He climbed on to the roof and cautiously stepped over to the skylight. He shattered the glass with a big rock and waited. No alarm. The man started to lower himself through the skylight when suddenly he got stuck. He attempted to escape, but the skylight was too small.

The next morning, the janitor arrived to clean the bank. "Oh my gosh!" he cried. He called the police. "There are two legs sticking out of the ceiling," he told them.

The police arrived in ten minutes and helped the poor robber get through the skylight. Then they escorted him to jail.

Silent Watcher

Ken kissed her good night at the front entry of the apartment block. Noreen walked down the hallway to Number 7 and unlocked her door. Stepping inside, she flicked on the light and hurried to the patio doors. She pulled back the sheers and peered out to the street. Ken was waiting for her signal before heading home himself.

He returned Noreen's wave and disappeared down the street. As she turned away from the window, a chill crept through her that had nothing to do with the March night. She saw what looked to be a person hiding behind the shrubs near the end of her building. Her heart beat faster as she ran back to the light switch. With the room darker now, Noreen again went to the patio doors to get a better look outside. Yes, there he was, almost hidden by the branches. He had on a winter hat of some sort and a scarf, from what she could make out.

Noreen began to pace, trying not to worry. After half an hour, she checked outside again. The figure was still at his post, not moving, just watching. She phoned Ken, who had just got home. "I'm scared, Ken, he's just standing there, watching my apartment!"

When Ken heard the rest of the details, he started to laugh. "The sun will look after your peeping Tom tomorrow, honey," he said. "I saw that guy as I left your place. It's a snowman!"

Supermarket Temptations

Do you ever go to the food store for a quart of milk and then end up leaving with a bag of groceries? Food stores are designed to tempt you to buy groceries. Careful shoppers know how to avoid being tempted by items they don't really need.

In most stores, the milk is located as far from the door as possible. That is because most shoppers buy milk. So the store owners want to make sure you have to walk past a lot of merchandise on your way to the dairy case. Along that route you'll also find snacks and baked goods. These are items that people are most likely to buy on impulse.

The ends of aisles are speed bumps. As you slow down to go around them, you may spot a stack of paper towels. Since they are out of their usual place, you may think they are on sale. Again, this is another way that store owners entice you to buy their products.

Giving in to temptation is hard on a budget. So it is important to learn ways to leave the store with your budget intact. Plan your weekly meals and then make up a grocery list. As you look for the items on the list, remember to be flexible. For example, if you've planned on buying cod for dinner, but it costs too much, opt for sole. Also, make a mental list of the standard prices of your usual purchases. By doing this, you will know a bargain when you see one. Finally, use coupons only for the items on your list. You aren't saving money if you use the coupons on foods you don't need in the first place.

Goalies

Hockey goalies have made a special place for themselves in sports. They are often called loners, or at least they prefer to be alone before, during, and after a game. They have superstitions. Some will talk only to certain players before a game, while others will let only some players tap their goal pads with a stick. Glenn Hall played over 500 consecutive games in his career and threw up before each one. Patrick Roy talks to his goal posts and steps over each line on the ice while skating to and from his net.

In the old days, goalies could not go down to stop a shot. They never wore masks, and they had no back-ups. If one of them was cut, the team doctor would stitch him up and put him back in the net. Once, in the Stanley Cup final, New York Rangers coach Lester Patrick had to play goal when his goalie could not return to the game. The Rangers won the cup.

Jacques Plante was the first goalie to wear a mask in a game. Consequently, he was called a sissy. His face had been cut, and his team still needed him, so he pulled out a mask and put it on.

Today, all goalies wear masks, but they still have plenty to be worried about. Players can shoot the puck over 60 miles per hour. The game is faster. Plus, goalies have additional responsibilities. They handle the puck now and make passes to clear the zone. They have even scored the odd goal.

Fire and a Friend

Howard crawled out of bed, quickly pulling on his blue jeans and ski jacket. Bare feet slid into chilly boots. Growling at the 6:05 a.m. clock face, he grabbed some matches from the dresser and shuffled to the furnace room.

The pilot light was out again. He crouched by the furnace and lit the match. The explosion threw him against the cement wall. Angry flames surrounded him, but his ears were deaf to their roar. His nose and throat burned with smoke and heat as he tried to breathe. Everything was out of place. Howard was alone and trapped!

Howard blindly fought through the blaze. Finally reaching the outdoors, he gratefully threw himself into the coolness of the snow.

The injured man squinted toward the lights of a house just across the railway tracks. Ed would be having his morning coffee. As Howard stumbled to the crossing, he saw with horror that a train blocked his path.

"If I crawl under it, it may start moving and run over me," Howard spoke to himself. "I'll have to climb between the cars."

His body painfully worked over the iron connection. The skin from the palms of his hands stayed on the cold metal joint. Wheezing at the door of Ed's house, Howard kicked it with a charred boot.

Ed saw a shape that didn't even look human, whispering, "Help!" The stranger's face was a puffy mask. His hair and parts of his ears were burned off. His jacket was a collar with a zipper, and two wrist bands above blistered hands.

As Ed drove the suffering man to the hospital, he wondered if this brave stranger would live. Ed didn't know he had just saved his friend's life.

The Star Witness

The FBI agent burst into the chief's office.

"We've got them! Baker, Maffie, Pino – the whole stinking lot. O'Keefe confessed everything. I cannot believe how good these crooks were. They were casing the building, making plans, walking in and out of that place for two years. They knew everything – security systems, schedules, who turned what light on when. You want to know how they got inside?"

The agent flipped through his tattered notebook.

"There it is. They removed the door locks, replaced them with bogus locks, and brought the locks to some locksmith on the other side of Boston. He made keys for the locks, and once they had the keys, they went back into the building and replaced the bogus locks with the original locks. Nobody suspected. These guys were crawling around the place for two years, and nobody suspected a thing! The Brinks building, for God's sakes! It's the safest building in Boston."

"Why confess now, after six years?" asked the chief.

"O'Keefe feels the other gang members ripped him off," said the agent. "He never got his money. They unloaded pieces of the get-away truck in a dump near his house. He feels he's on his own. He said – and I quote – they all agreed that if anyone messed up, they would be 'taken care of.' O'Keefe figures they messed up. Talking to us is his way of taking care of them."

The Chief sighed, then smiled. "Let's finish this," he said.

High Blood Pressure

High blood pressure increases the risk of heart disease and stroke. The "silent killer" is a name given to high blood pressure. This is because people who have it do not feel sick. A person may suffer from the condition for years without feeling any different at all. So people need to have their blood pressure checked each year by a doctor.

Blood pressure that is 140/90 or above is high. The first number, 140, is the force of the blood in the arteries when the heart is pumping blood out. The second number, 90, is the force of the blood in the arteries when the heart is filling with blood. Blood pressure varies with the time of day, activity, and stress. So it should be measured at least three times to make sure that the result is accurate.

Women and men are at special risk for developing high blood pressure if they come from families with a history of this condition. There are also certain times in a woman's life that may cause high blood pressure. Pregnant women can experience this condition in the last three months before delivery. Also, after menopause, women are more likely to suffer from high blood pressure than are men the same age.

There are some warning signs that indicate high blood pressure. A person may feel tired and dizzy. As well, a person may get headaches and a lot of nosebleeds. Other symptoms include a ringing in the ears and a flushed face.

High blood pressure can be prevented or controlled in a number of ways. People should use less salt in cooking and at the table. Instead, food should be seasoned with herbs and spices. Eating garlic can also help to reduce blood pressure. People should avoid smoking and limit their use of alcohol. Lastly, exercise such as walking or biking has been known to bring high blood pressure down to normal. Exercise will also assist weight loss. This, in turn, will lower blood pressure. If these methods do not work, drugs might be needed.

Hanukkah

Hanukkah is a Jewish holiday that lasts for eight days during December. Jews celebrate a victory that took place more than 2000 years ago. A foreign power ruled the country. The temple was in the hands of the foreign army. It was the most holy place of the Jews and the center of their religion. Judah the Maccabee led a small group of Jews. They opposed the Greek armies and recaptured the temple.

The Jews felt that the temple had been defiled by the foreigners. It had to be cleaned and purified with rituals. It had to be dedicated to the service of God again. They went to relight the holy lamp in the temple, but there was only a small jar that held enough oil for one day. However, a miracle kept the lamp alight for eight days. These eight days marked the first Hanukkah celebration.

Hanukkah is called the Festival of the Lights. A menorah, which holds eight candles plus a "helper" candle, is lit every night. The eight candles stand for the eight days of Hanukkah. On the first night, the head of the family uses the helper candle to light one of the candles. Every evening, one more candle is lit. The candles burn for about half an hour. While they are burning, no one is supposed to do any work. After the lighting of the candles, there are special prayers to recall the brave Hebrews who fought to recover their country and the temple.

Some children receive money, which is called "Hanukkah Gelt," on the first day of the holiday. Other children get chocolate coins wrapped in gold foil. Small gifts are also exchanged during the holiday. The children play with a wooden spinning top that is called a driedl. The four sides of the top are marked with four Hebrew letters that stand for the words "A great miracle happened there."

All families eat special foods, such as latkes, during the Hanukkah celebration. Latkes are potato pancakes fried in oil.

Midnight Intruder

A number of break-ins had occurred in the Milton's neighborhood. With her husband away on business, Susan was afraid for her young son and herself. After the late news on TV that night, she locked all the doors and windows and made sure the timer light was set. For her own peace of mind, a baseball bat stood near her bed.

The next morning, Susan awoke to sun shining through her bedroom window and a squirming toddler attempting to get under the covers. She scooped Tommy up with a kiss and marched to the kitchen for breakfast. As she turned to the stove, the smile faded and her mouth went dry. The wooden lid of the glass cookie jar lay silently on the counter. How had that happened? Tommy was too small to reach that high, and there were no telltale crumbs on his fuzzy pajamas.

That night Susan took a long time to fall asleep, but at 1:30 a.m. her eyes flew open as she held her breath and listened closely. Someone was rattling the elements on the stove! Hearing a scraping noise at the sink, she grabbed the bat and tiptoed to the kitchen. A floorboard creaked beneath her just as she lunged through the doorway with the bat poised above her, ready to strike the intruder. The night light dimly lit an empty kitchen, the cookie jar lid on the counter, and a knife in the sink. Susan was trembling with fear and relief.

Wednesday night Susan was ready for the prowler, with her movie camera set to film the counter between the stove and sink. Drifting off to sleep, she heard it again – someone was in the kitchen! Half an hour passed as she tightly gripped the bat and prayed the intruder would leave. When Susan was sure there were no more sounds from the kitchen, she crept out to view the crime video.

Captured on tape, the culprit turned out to be a mouse, with the amazing ability to work the lid off the cookie jar whenever he pleased!

Greta's Vigil

Greta paid for the hotel room. She carried her luggage to the second floor corner room, just as she had done for 28 years. The room was a bit more expensive now. Each year, the price went up a little, and the quality of the hotel lessened. But she expected that. The years had not been kind to her either.

When she was a bride those many years ago, her groom had gently lifted her and carried her over the threshold of Number 3 suite. Greta closed her eyes and hugged her body, recalling how her arms and his fit perfectly around each other, and how much the couple was in love. How she longed now to feel his embrace. There was a wonderful scent about Philip, she recalled. Was she dreaming, or did she smell that sweet odor right now?

That bright, starlit night in May lived in Greta's memory as clearly as if it had been just yesterday. Many gray hairs and unwanted wrinkles had appeared since then. She hoped Philip would still find her attractive. From her suitcase, she produced a framed snapshot of a smiling wedding couple. Yes, she had changed quite a lot since that photo was taken. She laid out her lacy nightgown on the tattered bedspread. She carefully placed a red rose upon the pillow as she turned back the covers. Greta heard her lover say, "We need champagne! I'll be right back, darling. This is to be a special evening. By the way, did I mention I love you more than life itself?" She felt a gentle kiss brush her lips, and he was gone – just as it had been 28 years ago.

Greta waited for his return, as she did on each anniversary of her wedding and of her husband's death.

Food Poisoning

In the United States, there are over 14 million cases of food poisoning each year. This condition is caused by germs. Salmonella is a common germ found in meat, poultry, eggs, and egg products. The symptoms of salmonella food poisoning include nausea, stomach cramps, diarrhea, fever, and headache. These symptoms usually occur 6 to 72 hours after eating the food and can last from 3 to 5 days.

Food poisoning is caused by a chain of events. First, there must be germs, such as salmonella or E. coli, on the food. These germs need the right conditions to grow: warmth, moisture, and food. The germs grow best in a moist setting where the temperature ranges between 41 to 140 degrees Fahrenheit. The germs also need a food source, such as dairy and egg products, meat, poultry, or fish, in order to grow and multiply. In ideal conditions, one germ can multiply to 2,097,152 within 7 hours.

The best defense against food poisoning is to take the offensive – to work actively to prevent it. Cooked or refrigerated foods, such as potato salad, should not sit at room temperature for more than two hours. The last items that shoppers should pick up are frozen foods, along with those that can perish. These items should be placed in the fridge and freezer as soon as possible. As the temperature of food goes down, so does the risk of organisms growing in it.

Heat kills most germs, even the hardy E.coli. But, for this to happen, all parts of the food must reach 158 degrees Fahrenheit. If microwaves are used, it is important to turn the food several times so that it is evenly heated. Food such as eggs, meat, and fish should never be eaten raw. For instance, raw eggs should not be used in Caesar salads or eggnog.

Food is contaminated through poor handling and lack of personal hygiene by those who prepare and serve it. It is important to wash hands with soap and warm water before food is prepared and after using the bathroom. During food preparation, hands, knives, and equipment such as cutting boards can become infected with germs from raw food such as meat. If the same equipment and knives are used to prepare another dish, such as carrots, the second dish can become infected with germs from the raw food. If the carrots are not cooked again before being eaten, the germs will not be killed. So it is a good idea to use separate cutting boards for meats and vegetables. From time to time, cutting boards should be soaked in bleach. By following these simple guidelines, one can avoid food poisoning.

Finishing the Railroad

British Columbia became part of Canada in 1871. Before that, it was a colony of Britain. The mountains created a barrier between the West Coast and the rest of the country, restricting the travel and trade between them. It was easier for people on the coast to trade with the United States, as most river valleys lay south and north between ranges of mountains. As well, travel along the coast by ship was much faster than travelling overland to the East.

American people living on the West Coast had much in common with British Columbians: mining, logging, ocean products, and shipping were important to both. The Americans wanted the colony and wanted B.C. to join the United States. The Prime Minister of Canada dreamed of a "vast dominion" stretching from sea to sea that included B.C. He promised the people of the West Coast a railroad to connect B.C. to the rest of Canada, assuring them it would be finished within ten years. British Columbia agreed to enter into Confederation on the condition that railway construction would commence in two years and be completed in ten.

The railway was a very expensive and daunting project. A train can move uphill on a shallow grade, but it cannot pull itself up mountains. Sometimes the railway had to go through the rock instead of around it. In certain places, whole pieces of mountain were blasted out of the way by explosives. The flying pieces of rock sometimes caused landslides or killed workers. The railway had to follow river valleys as much as possible. Many men drowned while building bridges over swift rivers. Six hundred trestles and bridges were constructed, and 27 tunnels were blasted through solid rock.

It was almost impossible to recruit enough workers to do this strenuous, perilous work. The railway company brought almost 9000 men via ship from China to construct the section of track through the mountains. These men came seeking to make a lot of money, yet they were paid less than the other workers. Some hoped to acquire land and remain in Canada. The Chinese workers often performed the hardest and most hazardous tasks. Before the railway was completed, over 600 had died in explosions and other accidents.

In 1885 the railroad joining British Columbia to the rest of the country was completed. Few Chinese men remained in Canada because the government refused to let Chinese women or their families enter the country. Moreover, the workers were not welcome to stay. It was an unfortunate chapter in Canadian history.

Tracking a Killer

The dumpster was blackened but already cool to the touch. A dark stain extended from the bottom corner down onto the pavement of the parking lot. When the police first removed the metal cover of the dumpster, they saw nothing in the charred interior but a layer of ash covering the bottom. Looking again, they distinguished a body so badly burned they could not tell whether it was animal or human. They transferred the fragile remains of the body to a body bag and sent them to a pathology lab. The pathologist established that the victim was human – a white female in her early twenties. X-rays revealed a gunshot to the head.

Three days after the discovery of the body, the police received a call from a local bank teller. The teller told them that a nervous young woman had come into the bank to close her account, but then left suspiciously before the transaction was completed. The teller had asked her to wait while she confirmed the withdrawal, but the woman was already gone when the teller returned. The woman – and a man who had been waiting for her just outside the bank doors – were recorded clearly by the bank's video security system. The police made a copy of the video and broadcast it on the local news station. Someone came forward and identified the woman. When questioned, the woman said the man who had accompanied her to the bank offered her $500. To earn this money, she needed to pose as a friend of his and withdraw all the money from this friend's account. The woman knew nothing about a murder.

The male friend was questioned and his vehicle inspected thoroughly. The police discovered bloodstains on the rear and right side of the car, and a bloody tire iron and a .22 calibre gun hidden in the trunk. The police knew they had their murderer, but they had to make a concrete connection between him and the victim. They went back to the pathologist. The pathologist prepared two DNA profiles – one with cells from a molar extracted from the victim's jaw and another using cells obtained from the bloodstains found on the suspect's car. The profiles matched.

Confronted by the evidence, the suspect confessed. He said the victim had owed him money but refused to pay. One night the suspect offered the victim a ride home from a bar. He beat her, put her body in the trunk of his car, drove to the deserted industrial park, threw the victim in the dumpster, shot her in the head, and set her on fire using gasoline. He was convicted of second-degree murder and sentenced to life imprisonment.

Not Bad for Forty!

Carla's birthday marked her 40th year of life. But had she really lived, she thought? She had heard others talk enthusiastically of holidays in Mexico. Impulsively, she booked an all-inclusive package to Mazatlan. She'd skip Christmas and all the hassle that went along with it. Her friend Marni agreed to accompany her.

The departure date saw two very excited women board the charter jet in -22 degree temperatures. The four-hour plane trip went quickly enough as Carla enjoyed the meal and a movie from her window seat. The Mexican resort was everything she had hoped it would be. The hotel was terrific, the food fantastic, and the weather hot! A constant wind blew from the Pacific Ocean, cooling the sunbathers by hotel pools and on sandy beaches. Vendors approached the basking tourists with every description of merchandise.

Carla and Marni had their hair braided and beaded by petite senoritas. They strolled the narrow sidewalks, stopping at shops and booths along the way. Little white golf-cart style cabs were cheap, enjoyable transportation, taking the adventurous duo to the world's highest lighthouse, the fishing docks, the cruise ship ports, and the famed fiestas of Mexican night life.

The week sped by. Carla held an iguana to pose for a picture on the beach, tried lobster for the first time ever, and topped it off with an exhilarating airborne escapade – parasailing. She was amazed at how fearlessly she slipped into the harness gear, receiving brief instruction in broken English. "Sit down like you sit on a toilet. Then run, but stay sitting..."

Easily said, a little awkward to accomplish! However the sky was hers as a motorboat gently towed the parachute into the wind and up over the ocean! The shoreline's many hotels were distinct in their shapes and colors. Thatched palm roofs of shade huts along the beach looked like little mushrooms sprouting from a sandy bed. Other brilliantly colored parasails dotted the sky in the distance. Ten minutes later, Carla spotted the instructor's flag, waving her in for the landing. She tugged the rope sling above her right arm, and the chute eased her down to earth again. "Ha!" she congratulated herself, "How's that for 40?"

Carla was extremely happy! She felt confident, content, and a little bit crazy as she sipped margaritas and counted her blessings.

Baldness

The medical term used to describe permanent baldness is alopecia. The more common term is pattern baldness. Pattern baldness or permanent hair loss strikes men more than women. In fact, two out of three men develop some type of balding during their lifetime. For males, this condition tends to result in a receding hairline and baldness on the crown of the head. For females, pattern baldness is the thinning of hair over the entire scalp. Permanent hair loss is largely hereditary among both men and women. So if a person's ancestors were bald, chances are he or she will inherit the trait.

Hair loss can be temporary or permanent. Factors linked with short-term hair loss include stress, hormonal imbalance, an underactive or overactive thyroid, and chemotherapy. Diets that are low in protein or iron are also a factor. As well, women may experience short-term hair loss from menopause, the stress of childbirth, or as a side effect of using birth control pills.

In our society, a great deal of emphasis is placed on one's appearance. Consequently, watching a hairline recede can be traumatic. Pattern baldness has been known to affect one's self-esteem, motivation, self-image, and ultimately happiness. Many people who experience hair loss spend lots of time and attention, not to mention huge sums of money, to find a treatment or a cure.

There are several treatments for pattern baldness. An American organization called the Food and Drug Administration (FDA) approved a drug marketed as Rogaine, which is available over the counter. Rogaine is a lotion that is rubbed into the scalp twice a day. Its effectiveness varies, and research shows that 25 to 30 percent of men experience some hair regrowth. The product seems to be most effective in early stages of hereditary baldness.

In 1998, the FDA approved Propecia, the first pill to treat male pattern hair loss effectively. In studies of 1,553 men, 86 percent of those taking the drug grew new hair or maintained their hair. This pill can be used only by men, as it poses a threat of birth defects among pregnant women. Like all prescription drugs, Propecia may cause side effects such as less desire for sex, difficulty in achieving an erection, and a decrease in the amount of semen.

Surgery is another alternative. Hair transplants are usually performed by dermatologists. They take tiny plugs of skin, each containing several hairs, from the back or side of the head. The plugs are then implanted into bald sections of scalp. Three or four transplants may be needed, at four-month intervals. Risk of infection is relatively high in this form of hair replacement. Another drawback of surgery is that this type of treatment is expensive and can also be very painful.

Why Can Birds Fly?

Only three groups of animals – birds, insects and bats – have acquired the power of true flight; that is, flight in which the wings are flapped rhythmically up and down to produce lift and thrust.

All fliers have to overcome similar problems. Air is such a thin medium, compared with water or earth, that travellers passing through it must have light bodies and wings to be able to maintain lift. They must also have a high "power/weight ratio." That is, their flight muscles must be extremely powerful in relation to their body weight. A pigeon's heart muscles, which operate its wings, account for more than a third of its body weight.

Birds have remarkably light skeletons. This lightness has been achieved without sacrificing strength. The skull bones of modern birds are very thin, and heavy teeth have been replaced by light, horny beaks. Long bones, such as those in the wings, are hollow, supported by a criss-crossing system of internal struts. The tail, which helps with steering, is formed entirely of that skin covering unique to birds – feathers.

Extremely light, flexible, and airproof, feathers are a miracle of flight technology. A "primary" or flight feather consists of a shaft or quill, hollow at its base for conveying nourishment, solid towards its tip for strength; and a vane made up of side shafts called barbs. These barbs, in turn, support rows of barbules, equipped with interlocking hooks to form a fine mesh surface for the feather. If the barbules break apart, the bird can reset them by preening, an important task which occupies much of a bird's time. Near the base of the tail, a bird has oil glands, the oil being used during preening and cleaning to coat the feathers, keeping them waterproof and buoyant. Together with the tail feathers, the primary feathers form an arched wing that provides lift and thrust, or reverse thrust when landing.

Birds require a complex nervous system to remain stable in flight. For this reason birds have relatively larger brains than all mammals (except primates), and the part of the brain that coordinates movement in particularly well developed.

Flying uses a lot of energy. Consequently, birds spend much of their time searching for food. Oxygen is also needed in large amounts, and birds have quite uniquely designed lungs with special air sacs, which surround the vital organs of the body and even penetrate certain wing bones. Inside these sacs, the air flows around a one-way system, enabling the bird to extract all the oxygen from one breath of air while at the same time expelling all carbon dioxide. The air sacs also allow the bird to lose the excessive heat produced during flight, and as a bonus, they reduce the density or solidity of its body.

The Suspect

They say the father searched the grounds of the estate desperately. He called the state police; and instantly droves of police, investigators, and reporters descended on the secluded mansion, possibly obliterating important evidence that might have been left behind. The investigators did find a rough, home-made ladder; a chisel; and a ransom note demanding $50,000, which they found on the window sill of the second-floor library – the last place where the parents claimed they had seen their 20-month-old son.

For a month, letters poured in – psychic predictions, death threats, and sympathy notes. The parents withdrew from sight in an attempt to avoid the constant curiosity of the public. A retired principal came forward saying that he had been in contact with the kidnapper and would act as an intermediary. He explained that because of a strong personal desire to see the kidnapped baby reunited with the parents, he had invested a thousand dollars of his own money in a newspaper ad that encouraged the kidnapper to contact him.

In April, one month after the abduction, the father and the retired principal met in a cemetery with the kidnapper. The principal handed the kidnapper $50,000 in marked bills and returned to the parked car where the father of the child waited anxiously. He produced a note that said the toddler was in a boat off the coast of Massachusetts. The information proved false. One month later, only a few miles away from the family mansion, a truck driver pulled over to the side of a country lane to relieve himself. He discovered the tiny body of the missing boy hidden under a pile of dead leaves – his skull fractured.

Two long years later, a traveller stopped at a gas station, purchased his gas with a single bill, and drove away. The proprietor of the gas station, suspecting that the bill might be counterfeit, jotted down the traveler's license plate number on the back of it and promptly reported the incident to the police. The bill turned out to be one of the marked bills from the cemetery transaction two years earlier. The license plate number led the police to the residence of a German-born carpenter with a criminal record, residing illegally in the United States. Further investigation led to the discovery of $14,000 hidden in the garage and a missing plank of wood from the attic floor. Was this man the kidnapper? The media and the public, after clamoring for justice for over two years, were ready to believe so. When the retired principal testified in court that the suspect was the man to whom he had given the $50,000 in the cemetery, the suspect's fate was sealed.

In spite of numerous doubts concerning the purely circumstantial evidence provided at the trial, Bruno Hauptman died in the electric chair in the spring of 1936, charged with kidnapping Charles Lindbergh Jr. – the child of the famous and beloved aviator, Charles Lindbergh.

Remembering Emily

An elderly man trudged along the dusty incline of a path that led to the knoll overlooking Newdale. For most of his life he had lived in the rolling landscape, near the southern boundaries of this rural village.

Now he looked down on his hometown to see the busy profile of a country fair, beckoning him toward its sounds and smells. Lucas Wicks gripped his walking cane with renewed strength and made his way down the slope. With each step, a memory crept into his aging mind.

Little Emily had been at the fair that day, 25 years ago. Lucas and his wife Margaret were busy at the jewellery store until late that afternoon. Emily pleaded, with her four-year-old insistence, until her parents conceded. "Very well, Emily. You must behave, and listen to what your Uncle Morris says," Lucas recalled his wife having chided. Morris was Margaret's younger brother and not of a responsible nature.

Emily's blonde ringlets bounced as she eagerly counted out her piggy bank money to buy cotton candy and ride tickets. The silver carnival charm bracelet, designed by her adoring father, jangled on her chubby wrist.

"Good-bye, Daddy." She kissed his cheek for the last time.

"You all right, Luke?" a voice interrupted the jeweller's thoughts. Lucas hadn't realized he'd reached the fairground gates and was standing mesmerized by the spinning ferris wheel. He positioned his portly frame on a nearby bench and answered his neighbor. "Sure Arty, just a little overheated." He wiped the sweat off his forehead with a swipe of his arm.

Resting in the shade, Lucas again drifted into the past. His precious Emily had been kidnapped that day, at this very fairground. Years of investigation had never developed a successful lead as to her whereabouts, and Lucas had never forgiven his brother-in-law for his incompetence in caring for his rambunctious niece that fateful day. Margaret had taken her own life only months later. Lucas had dejectedly continued at his jewellery store until his retirement five years ago. From his watchband sparkled a tangible memory of his treasured daughter–a tiny carousel charm that was the identical mate to one he had crafted for his child. Suddenly a gentle tap on his shoulder pulled Lucas from his reverie. He raised tired eyes to see a vision. Before him stood the replica of his unforgettable Emily. Golden curls cascaded around rosy cheeks. The cherub pointed to the awestruck senior's wristwatch.

"I have a merry-go-round just like you," she chortled, holding out her arm to display the unique charm bracelet Lucas had designed many years before. Behind the child stood her mother, so unmistakable was the likeness. Hardly daring to hope, Lucas rose slowly from the bench. "Emily, is it you?" he whispered. He thought he saw a momentary glimmer of recognition in her eyes. "No, my name is Mary," she answered as she gathered up her child and turned to go.

Beans

The benefits of beans have been recognized since people first began to cultivate their food. In the Middle East beans were cultivated about 8000 B.C., and in China soybeans were cultivated earlier than 3000 B.C. Beans were very popular in ancient Greece and Rome. In fact, they were used for counting votes in ancient Rome. Beans have been eaten around the world for over 10,000 years and are still a staple in many countries.

Bean dishes are eaten daily by the majority of the people throughout the Middle East, North Africa, and South and Central America. In East Asia soybeans are used extensively, mostly in the forms of bean curd, miso, and tamari. Bean curd, which is produced from soybean milk, and tamari, a naturally fermented soy sauce, are used throughout East Asia. Miso, a fermented soybean paste, is used as a soup base and a seasoning mainly in Japan.

Beans, an important source of nutrients, contain iron, B vitamins, folic acid, calcium, magnesium, and potassium and are the best plant source of protein. This food source is high in dietary fibre, low in saturated fat, and cholesterol-free. Dried beans are also a healthy food choice because they are not subjected to the preservatives or other chemicals generally used in processed foods.

Beans are so pretty and decorative that people are tempted to line them up in glass jars on a countertop. This temptation should be resisted, however, as beans stay fresher longer when they are stored in a dark place. Ideally, beans should be stored in glass bottles or plastic bags in a cupboard or drawer located as far as possible from the oven – in the coolest, driest place in the kitchen. The beans should be consumed within six months, as older beans absorb more water during the cooking process and take longer to become tender.

Although beans are very nutritious, many people tend to avoid them because they produce gas. The bean contains sugars, which are at the root of the intestinal problems attributed to beans. The stomach does not contain the enzymes needed to digest these sugars in the small intestine, so the sugars arrive in the large intestine undigested. The bacteria that live in the large intestine feed off and ferment these sugars, producing carbon dioxide, hydrogen, and a few other gases as by-products.

There are a few ways to reduce 60 percent of the gas produced from the sugars in beans. Soaking the beans in water permits the gas-producing sugars to be released. Gas is also reduced by discarding the water that the beans are soaked in, and by changing the water that beans are cooked in after 40 minutes. As well, a product marketed as Beano, which is available in most supermarkets and pharmacies, reduces gas production, as it contains an enzyme that assists in the digestion of sugars.

Women and Osteoporosis

Osteoporosis, a condition of decreased bone mass, is one of the most common diseases affecting women. It leads to fragile bones that are at an increased risk of fracture. As the disease progresses, the spinal column can decrease in length, causing a height loss of several inches. The spine can also become curved as a result of fractures caused by the pressure of body weight on the deteriorating vertebrae.

The term "porosis" means spongy, which describes the appearance of osteoporosis bones when they are broken in half to examine them. Normal bone marrow has small holes within it, but a bone with osteoporosis will have much larger holes. Decreased bone mass is mainly caused by a decrease in the calcium content of the bones.

Those with the highest risk factor for osteoporosis are usually slender, small-boned Caucasian or Asian women who have exercised very little and taken in insufficient calcium during their growing years. The profile of women at risk also includes those who smoke and drink alcohol excessively. Finally, the chances of osteoporosis seem to increase dramatically with age, since a woman's bone mass normally peaks at age 35, after which she tends to lose about 1 percent of bone mass per year.

Osteoporosis is different from most other diseases or common illnesses in that there is no one single cause. The overall health of a person's bones is a function of many factors, ranging from how well the bones were formed in youth to the level of exercise the bones have seen over the years. One prevailing theory maintains that the disease results from a loss of the female hormone estrogen. This loss affects the calcium content of bones. Therefore, menopause and the removal of ovaries or uterus may lead to osteoporosis.

Osteoporosis can usually be prevented with some simple lifestyle changes. Regular and frequent weight-bearing exercise is one of the best strategies for increasing bone mass. Running, walking, and weight-lifting stimulate bone-cell production. Most doctors recommend about thirty minutes of exercise about three to five times per week.

As this disease often originates in a calcium deficiency, women should pay special attention to their calcium intake. The daily recommended dietary calcium intake varies by age, sex, and menopausal status. If women have difficulty consuming dairy products, there are other calcium-rich foods that should be included in their diet. Beans, especially kidney and pinto, and tofu are rich in calcium and protein. Good sources of calcium also include broccoli, nuts, figs, prunes, salmon, sardines, and leafy greens. Vitamins C and D increase the body's absorption of calcium. Coffee and tea should be avoided, as they promote the excretion of calcium through the urine.

For women at menopause, the appropriate administration of estrogen is the most potent means by which bone mass may be preserved. In fact, correction of low reproductive hormone levels at any age is important if proper bone mass is to be maintained. There is no one treatment or combination of treatments that can guarantee zero risk of fractures due to osteoporosis. The best prevention, however, is a life-long commitment to physical activity, good nutrition, and normal reproductive hormone status.

The Big One

The men spilled silently from the 1949 green Ford truck parked at the far end of the playground, which adjoined the building, and waited. Nobody spoke, but they were deeply aware of each other's constant upward glances, the slow, steadying intakes of breath, the subtle shifting of weight from one foot to the other and back again. When a quick flash of light from the roof of a tenement building overlooking the targeted building pierced the evening sky, the seven armed men moved in unified silence through the playground and down the quiet street until they huddled momentarily in the darkened entrance of the building. Using the copy of the outside door key that they had previously obtained from an unsuspecting locksmith, the gloved men entered quickly, donning their Halloween masks and chauffeur caps. Wordlessly, they made their way directly to the vault room on the second floor, where they knew five employees were engaged in their nightly chore of checking and storing the payrolls and deliveries that had been entrusted to their care that day. They unlocked the vault room door with one of the many other keys in their possession and easily overpowered the unsuspecting employees, expertly binding and gagging them with rope and adhesive tape.

The robbers moved through the room performing their assigned tasks silently, like dancers stepping effortlessly through a familiar choreography. The practiced routine was interrupted only once, but completely unexpectedly, by the sound of a warning buzzer. One of the robbers quickly removed the adhesive tape from the mouth of one employee and learned that the buzzer indicated that someone wanted access to the vault area. Two of the other gang members immediately positioned themselves near the sole door in the room, guns poised, ready to nab the intruder. For some reason, the would-be victim strolled past the vault, seemingly unconcerned, so they let him be. The two gang members returned to their work, but instinctively they all moved more swiftly pushed by a stronger sense of urgency.

The gang loaded their hefty bags of loot into the waiting getaway vehicle, which was now parked according to schedule at the front entrance of the building. They clambered into the back of it, and as they made their escape, the five employees in the vault room worked themselves free and reported the crime. They didn't know it at the time, but they had just witnessed the crime of the century.

The robbers had succeeded in stealing $1.2 million in cash and $1.5 million in checks, money orders, and other securities from the "impenetrable" Brinks building at 165 Prince Street in Boston, Massachusetts. Total time of the heist? Less than five minutes.

Secret of Significance

Standing elegantly against the papered wall of Helen's massive bedroom, a lustrous maple armoire gleamed in silent splendor. Helen was still basking in the pleasure of finding such a treasure abandoned in a dusty corner of the Ericksons' farmhouse attic. The retiring couple had gladly parted with the monstrosity that had been a gift to Daniel Erickson's mother, Edna. "Mom said the cabinetmaker was an old acquaintance and the wardrobe was the only thing she'd ever really owned." Daniel shook his head sadly, remembering how cruelly his father had treated his mother and himself. "Father despised the thing and insisted it be out of sight immediately after Mom passed away over thirty-five years ago."

Helen was appalled that a quality piece of craftsmanship should be hated and hidden by the elder Mr. Erickson, but elated that the immaculately polished antique was now in her possession. Carefully she measured and clipped rectangles of lavender scented drawer liners before placing her own personal items into their historical time capsule. Blouses, scarves, jewelry, journals, and stationery – each had a fragrant storage spot. Removing the bottom drawer, she noticed a yellowed sheet of parchment flutter to the floor. The edges were brittle, but the writing appeared barely faded as Helen reached for the letter addressed to Edna Abernathy. Blushing, she realized the object of her curiosity was indeed a love letter to the deceased Mrs. Erickson. She envisioned a young woman dressed in the fashion of 1931, as indicated by the date in the upper corner of the document. Helen nestled into a gigantic wooden rocker near the window, and journeyed into the past through the author's captivating letter…

My beloved Edna,

How my heart and being yearns for you as your wedding day approaches. My future is dismal and worthless without your tenderness, beauty, passion, and companionship. This dastardly villain to whom you are betrothed is sure to make our lives miserable and destitute. It wrenches my heart to know your father is merely satisfying his greed with this arrangement, and it is beyond my power to alter it.

I have lovingly constructed an armoire for you to remember me by, built with some significance. Seven drawers represent the months of love we shared, and each shall house the secret of our affair. The tightly grained maple wood shall remind you of our embraces as you caress its smoothness with your gentle fingers. Its pleasant aroma is reminiscent of the fragrant forest floor on which we reclined to contemplate the starlit skies and our unfulfilled future. The rod supporting your garments has been hewn from the strongest of branches, one that reached to the heavens; through this column, your sweetness shall be transported to me. Each hinge and handle is of brass – an alloy of strength, pliability, and beauty; this is our love for each other even in separate lives. Engraved above, below, and upon its door are complicated symbols of lions, for which you shall have a lifetime of memories. My request, before taking my own life, is that you name our son Daniel, for he shall have lions to battle.

I shall be waiting, my precious Edna,

Yours in life and in death,

Sullivan McMasters

Section Five

Graded Word List

Instructor's Note
The highest level at which the student recognizes 90% of the words in a column should be the starting point for administration of the passages. (If the student scores 90 to 100% at Level 1, the starting point should be the Level 1 easy passages.) Stop when the student misses 3 words in any one column.

1

which _____

around _____

mother _____

something _____

thought _____

children _____

our _____

because _____

every _____

could _____

2

since _____

ocean _____

between _____

everyone _____

friend _____

beautiful _____

kitchen _____

question _____

eight _____

waited _____

3

neighbor _____

frightened _____

exclaimed _____

chief _____

farming _____

obey _____

removed _____

serious _____

prepared _____

alarm _____

4

laughter _____

impossible _____

knowledge _____

delicious _____

voyage _____

celebration _____

echo _____

hymn _____

nuisance _____

guarded _____

5

exhausted _____

transparent _____

poisonous _____

behavior _____

merchandise _____

considerable _____

deliberately _____

patience _____

investigate _____

threatened _____

6

fatigue _____

sympathize _____

accomplishment _____

yacht _____

strenuous _____

luxurious _____

occurrence _____

necessity _____

alcohol _____

isolation _____

7

testimonial   _____

synthetic   _____

maneuver   _____

pneumonia   _____

poise   _____

immune   _____

lyric   _____

prohibited   _____

siesta   _____

hysterical   _____

8

persuasive   _____

capillary   _____

commemorate   _____

conscientious   _____

jostle   _____

susceptible   _____

inquisitive   _____

pretentious   _____

affiliated   _____

rendezvous   _____

9

conscription   _____

recipient   _____

domicile   _____

diminutive   _____

euphoria   _____

exonerate   _____

nausea   _____

fictitious   _____

transactions   _____

nuptial   _____

Student's Passage: page 34

Introduction: This is a story about cats.

Cats

Some people have cats. Cats like to sleep. They can sleep all day. They like to sleep in the sun. Cats do not like to get wet. Cats like to eat meat. They like to drink milk. Cats are good pets.

(41 words)

RETELLING
Please retell the story.

COMPREHENSION

____ (F) What do cats like to do all day?
          (sleep)

____ (F) Where do cats like to sleep?
          (in the sun)

____ (F) What do cats not like?
          (water; to get wet – 1 out of 2)

____ (F) What do cats like to eat?
          (meat)

____ (F) What do cats like to drink?
          (milk)

READING LEVEL

Independent	Instructional	Frustration
$4\frac{1}{2}$ – 5 points	3 - 4 points	$2\frac{1}{2}$ points or less

PRIOR KNOWLEDGE
How much did you know about cats before reading this story?

I knew:

1 — nothing   2 — very little   3 — something   4 — a lot

LEVEL OF INTEREST
How much did you like reading this story?

1 — it was not interesting   2 — it was fairly good   3 — it was good   4 — it was excellent

Introduction: This passage is about ants.

Mary and her Son

Mary is mad. Her son is late. He is 14. He is out with his friends. Her son gets home at two. Mary gets mad at her son. Then her son gets mad. He says he is not a kid.

(40 words)

RETELLING
Please retell the story.

COMPREHENSION

___ (F)   Why is Mary mad?
           (her son is late)

___ (F)   How old is her son?
           (14)

___ (F)   Who did Mary's son go out with?
           (his friends)

___ (F)   What time did Mary's son get home?
           (two)

___ (I)   Why did Mary's son get mad?
           (He thought he was being treated like a kid;
           he wanted to stay out late – 1 out of 2)

READING LEVEL

Independent $4\frac{1}{2}$ – 5 points	Instructional 3 - 4 points	Frustration $2\frac{1}{2}$ points or less

LEVEL OF INTEREST
How much did you like reading this story?

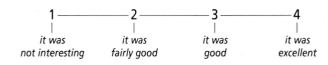

1	2	3	4
it was not interesting	*it was fairly good*	*it was good*	*it was excellent*

Student's Passage: page 36

Introduction: This is a story about Joe.

Joe Gets a Dog

Joe is sad. He is 68. He lives alone. He does not like to live alone. His friend

says get a dog. Joe gets a dog. Joe says his dog is his best friend.

(34 words)

RETELLING
Please retell the story.

COMPREHENSION

___ (F) How does Joe feel before he gets his dog?
(sad)

___ (I) Why do you think Joe is sad?
(he lives alone; he is lonely – 1 out of 2)

___ (F) How old is Joe?
(68)

___ (F) What does his friend say?
(get a dog)

___ (F) What does Joe say about his dog?
(it is his best friend)

READING LEVEL

Independent	Instructional	Frustration
$4\frac{1}{2}$ – 5 points	3 - 4 points	$2\frac{1}{2}$ points or less

LEVEL OF INTEREST
How much did you like reading this story?

1 ——————— 2 ——————— 3 ——————— 4

it was	it was	it was	it was
not interesting	fairly good	good	excellent

Student's Passage: page 37

Introduction: This is a story about Sam and Pat.

Sam and Pat

Sam went to the store. He had to get milk. He met Pat at the store. Pat had to get dog food. Sam liked Pat. He asked Pat out on a date. She said yes. Sam was very happy.

(39 words)

RETELLING

Please retell the story.

COMPREHENSION

___ (F)   Where did Sam go?
            (to the store)

___ (F)   What did Sam get at the store?
            (milk)

___ (F)   Who did Sam meet at the store?
            (Pat)

___ (F)   What did Pat buy at the store?
            (dog food)

___ (I)   Why do you think Sam was happy?
            (Pat said she would go out with him;
            Pat liked him – 1 out of 2)

READING LEVEL

Independent $4\frac{1}{2}$ – 5 points	Instructional 3 - 4 points	Frustration $2\frac{1}{2}$ points or less

LEVEL OF INTEREST

How much did you like reading this story?

1	2	3	4
it was not interesting	it was fairly good	it was good	it was excellent

Introduction: This is about losing body fat.

Losing Body Fat

It takes time to lose body fat. The key is to exercise and eat right. You need to exercise at least three times a week. Ride a bike. Go for a jog. Go for a swim. Walk the dog. Run up and down the stairs.

You should change the way you shop and eat. Look for fat-free foods in the store. Do not eat candy and chips. Eat lots of fish, grains, and fruit. Soon, you will begin to look slim and trim.

(84 words)

RETELLING
Please retell the story.

COMPREHENSION

____ (F) Name four kinds of exercise that the author suggested. *(biking; jogging; swimming; walking the dog; running up and down the stairs - 4 out of 5)*

____ (I) What do you think was the cheapest indoor exercise mentioned in this story? *(running up and down the stairs; walking the dog – 1 out of 2)*

____ (F) In order to lose weight, the story says you need to change the way you do two things. What should you change? *(the way you shop and eat)*

____ (F) What kind of food does the story say you should look for in the store? *(fat-free food)*

____ (I) Why should you not eat chips? *(they contain fat)*

____ (F) Name two types of food you should eat a lot of. *(fish; grains; fruit – 2 out of 3)*

READING LEVEL

Independent	Instructional	Frustration
6 points	4 - 5½ points	3½ points or less

PRIOR KNOWLEDGE
How much did you know about losing body fat before reading this story?

I knew:

1 — nothing   2 — very little   3 — something   4 — a lot

LEVEL OF INTEREST
How much did you like reading this story?

1 — it was not interesting   2 — it was fairly good   3 — it was good   4 — it was excellent

Introduction: This is about ants.

Ants

Most ants build their nests in soil and sand. Three kinds of ants live in the nest. The male ant mates with the queen. The queen ant lays the eggs. The worker ants have many jobs.

They watch the nest. They can bite and sting. The worker ants will fight until they die. An ant fight can last up to 16 hours. The worker ants hunt for food. They bring the food back to the nest. They also keep the nest clean.

(82 words)

RETELLING
Please retell the story.

COMPREHENSION

____ (F) Where do the ants build their nests?
Name two places. *(in soil and in sand)*

____ (F) Name three kinds of ants that live in the nest.
(worker ant, queen, and male ant)

____ (I) Which ant has the hardest job?
(the worker ant)

____ (F) How long can a fight last? *(16 hours)*

____ (I) How do you know that the worker ant is
brave? *(it will fight to its death; it will
fight for 16 hours - 1 out of 2)*

____ (F) The worker ant has many jobs. Name three
of them. *(clean the nest; watch the nest; hunt
for food; fight other ants; build the nest; bring
food back to the nest - 3 out of 6)*

READING LEVEL

Independent	Instructional	Frustration
6 points	4 - $5\frac{1}{2}$ points	$3\frac{1}{2}$ points or less

PRIOR KNOWLEDGE
How much did you know about ants before reading this story?

I knew:

1 — nothing 2 — very little 3 — something 4 — a lot

LEVEL OF INTEREST
How much did you like reading this story?

1 — it was not interesting 2 — it was fairly good 3 — it was good 4 — it was excellent

Introduction: This is about a woman's trip to a pawn shop.

The End

She went into the pawn shop. She said, "I need some money." He said, "What can you sell?" She showed him a ring and a watch.

"Take the ring," she said. "Are you sure?" he asked. "Yes. Take it." The man took the ring. He put it in a box.

Then the man gave the woman some money. He gave her $120. The woman took the money. Then the man gave the woman a ticket. The woman took the ticket. She began to cry.

(84 words)

RETELLING
Please retell the story.

COMPREHENSION

____ (I)   This story is called The End. What do you think is ending? *(a relationship had ended)*

____ (F)   What two things did the woman show the man? *(a ring and a watch)*

____ (I)   Do you think the man really wanted to take the ring from the woman? Explain your answer. *(no, he asked the woman if she was sure about giving him the ring; no, he felt sorry for her; no, he knew the ring was important to her - 1 out of 3)*

____ (F)   What did the man do with the ring? *(he took it and put it in a box)*

____ (F)   What two things did the woman do when the man gave her the ticket? *(she took the ticket and began to cry)*

____ (F)   How much money did the man give the woman? *($120)*

READING LEVEL

Independent	Instructional	Frustration
6 points	4 - 5½ points	3½ points or less

PRIOR KNOWLEDGE
Have you ever had experience with a pawn shop before?

1 —————— 2 —————— 3 —————— 4

no experience   very little   some experience   a lot of experience

LEVEL OF INTEREST
How much did you like reading this story?

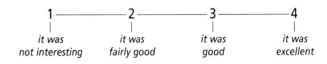

1 —————— 2 —————— 3 —————— 4

it was not interesting   it was fairly good   it was good   it was excellent

Introduction: This is the story of a criminal and a cop.

Ted and the Cop

The cop said, "Did you do it?" Ted just looked at him. Then the cop said,

"Where did you dump the body?" Ted just kept looking at him.

"We know you did it," said the cop. "Your friend told us." Ted just looked at

the cop. Ted thought, "Dumb cop. Cops are so dumb."

Then the cop turned off the tape recorder. "Get out!" he yelled. "Get out of

here!" Ted laughed at the cop. He laughed because he knew he would get

away with it.

(86 words)

RETELLING
Please retell the story.

COMPREHENSION

____ (F) How did the cop know that Ted dumped a
body? *(Ted's friend told the cop)*

____ (F) What did the cop do when Ted didn't say
anything? *(turned off the tape recorder;
yelled "Get out" – 1 out of 2)*

____ (I) Why do you think the cop let Ted go?
*(they didn't have the body; they didn't have
any proof that Ted was the murderer;
they didn't have any evidence - 1 out of 3)*

____ (I) How do you think the cop felt when Ted didn't
answer his questions? *(frustrated; angry; mad;
like a failure; upset - 1 out of 5)*

____ (F) Why did Ted laugh at the cop? *(he knew he
would get away with it)*

____ (I) What word would you use to tell what Ted
was like? *(cruel; evil; bad; clever; mean; cunning
smart; quiet - 1 out of 8)*

READING LEVEL

Independent	Instructional	Frustration
6 points	4 - 5½ points	3½ points or less

LEVEL OF INTEREST
How much did you like reading this story?

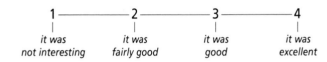

1 — 2 — 3 — 4
it was   *it was*   *it was*   *it was*
not interesting   *fairly good*   *good*   *excellent*

Student's Passage: page 42

Introduction: This is about HIV and AIDS.

AIDS

HIV is a virus. It is found in blood. It is found in semen. It is found in fluid from the vagina.

There are two ways men and women can get HIV. They can get HIV when they have sex with a person who has HIV. They can get HIV when they share needles with a person who has HIV.

At first, people with HIV feel fine. After a few years, people with HIV can start to get sick. HIV can turn into AIDS after two to ten years. When they have AIDS, their bodies cannot fight other diseases. Many people with AIDS have died.

There is no cure for AIDS. But people can prevent HIV. They can learn about the causes of HIV. Also, people can protect themselves. They can practice safe sex by using condoms. They can use clean needles.

(143 words)

RETELLING
Please retell the story.

COMPREHENSION

____ (F) Name three places where you can find HIV in the body. *(in blood, semen, and vaginal fluid)*

____ (F) Name two ways that a person can get HIV. *(when they have sex with a person who has HIV and when they share needles with a person who has HIV)*

____ (F) How long does it take HIV to turn into AIDS? *(two to ten years)*

____ (I) Why is HIV common among drug users? *(because they share dirty needles)*

____ (I) Why does a person with AIDS often get very sick with pneumonia or other diseases? *(because their body cannot fight other diseases; their immune system is weak –– 1 out of 2)*

____ (I) Can you get HIV from kissing someone? Explain your answer. *(no – HIV is not in saliva; HIV can only be passed through blood, semen, or vaginal fluid – 1 out of 2)*

____ (F) Name three ways people can prevent HIV. *(learn about the causes; protect themselves by practicing safe sex; use clean needles; use condoms – 3 out of 4)*

READING LEVEL

Independent 6½ - 7 points	Instructional 4½ - 6 points	Frustration 4 points or less

PRIOR KNOWLEDGE
How much did you know about AIDS before reading this story?

I knew:

1	2	3	4
nothing	very little	something	a lot

LEVEL OF INTEREST
How much did you like reading this story?

1	2	3	4
it was not interesting	it was fairly good	it was good	it was excellent

Student's Passage: page 43

Introduction: This is about polar bears.

The Polar Bear

Polar bears get most of their food from the ocean. Polar bears have a layer of blubber. It keeps them warm when they swim. The tiny webs between their toes help them swim.

The polar bear's coat is white. This colour makes it difficult for them to be seen on snow and ice. These bears have two layers of fur. The inner layer of fur is thick. This makes it hard for water to get to the skin. There is oil in their hair and skin. The oil helps to make them waterproof. They are the only bears with hair on the bottom of their feet. This hair keeps their feet warm. It keeps them from slipping on ice and snow.

(121 words)

RETELLING
Please retell the story.

COMPREHENSION

____ (F) Where do polar bears get most of their food from? *(the ocean)*

____ (F) What keeps the polar bear warm? *(blubber; hair on the bottom of their feet; inner layer of fur; two layers of fur – 1 out of 4)*

____ (F) Name two things that help to keep the polar bear dry. *(inner layer of fur; oil in their hair; oil in their skin – 2 out of 3)*

____ (F) What are two purposes for the hair on the bottom of their feet. *(it keeps them warm and it keeps them from slipping on ice and snow)*

____ (I) What do you think protects the polar bear from hunters? *(their white coat)*

____ (I) What do you think makes a polar bear different from all other bears? *(it has hair on the bottom of its feet; they are white; need to live in cold weather – 1 out of 3)*

____ (I) In what way is a polar bear like a duck? *(it has webbed feet; it has webs between its toes; it has oil to make skin waterproof – 1 out of 3)*

READING LEVEL

Independent 6½ - 7 points	Instructional 4½ - 6 points	Frustration 4 points or less

PRIOR KNOWLEDGE
How much did you know about polar bears before reading this story?

I knew:

1 — nothing 2 — very little 3 — something 4 — a lot

LEVEL OF INTEREST
How much did you like reading this story?

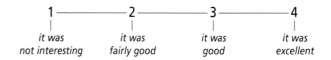

1 — it was not interesting 2 — it was fairly good 3 — it was good 4 — it was excellent

Student's Passage: page 44

Introduction: This story is about a man who got food poisoning.

Bad Food

Ron and Donna are husband and wife. Ron is a very big man. He is strong.

Donna is a small woman. She is a nurse.

One day Ron and Donna went out for dinner. Donna had a salad. Ron ate fish

and chips. Then they went to the zoo.

Ron got sick. His legs and arms were weak. He could not walk because of the

pain in his stomach. He was very hot. Then he was too cold. Donna knew Ron

had eaten some bad fish. She helped him to the car.

They drove to the hospital. The doctor said Ron had food poisoning. She gave

Ron some pills to make him better.

(113 words)

RETELLING
Please retell the story.

COMPREHENSION

_____ (F) What do Donna and Ron look like? *(Donna is small and Ron is very big)*

_____ (F) What did they eat for dinner? *(Donna ate a salad and Ron ate fish and chips)*

_____ (I) How did Donna know that Ron ate some bad fish? *(she was a nurse; he started feeling weak; he had a stomach pain; he was sick; he was hot and cold – 1 out of 5)*

_____ (F) What happened to Ron's body when he got sick? Name three things. *(his legs were weak; his arms were weak; he was hot; he was cold; he couldn't walk; he got a pain in his stomach – 3 out of 6)*

_____ (I) Why would it be hard for Donna to help Ron to the car? *(he was a big man; she was a small woman; he couldn't walk – 1 out of 3)*

_____ (I) Do you think Ron almost died from food poisoning? Explain your answer. *(no, his stomach wasn't pumped; no, he wasn't hospitalized; no, the doctor just gave him pills – 1 out of 3)*

_____ (I) Do you think the zoo was open during the evenings? Explain your answer. *(yes, because they went after dinner)*

READING LEVEL

Independent 6½ points	Instructional 4½ - 6 points	Frustration 4 points or less

PRIOR KNOWLEDGE
Have you ever had an experience with food poisoning before?

1 —————— 2 —————— 3 —————— 4

no experience   very little   some experience   a lot of experience

LEVEL OF INTEREST
How much did you like reading this story?

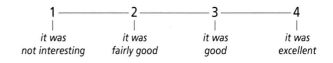

1 —————— 2 —————— 3 —————— 4

it was not interesting   it was fairly good   it was good   it was excellent

Student's Passage: page 45

Introduction: This is about a graduation night trick.

Rock and Roll

It was grad night. Steve was all dressed up for the dance. He was in a hurry. He jumped into his truck. Steve knew he was running late. As his truck pulled away from the curb, he heard a noise from below it. He was driving at a slow speed. His truck was rocking and rolling like a ride at the fair.

Steve stopped the truck. He swore under his breath. In his fancy suit, he got down on his knees. Steve looked under his truck. He saw what was wrong. A rock was attached to the drive shaft with wire. Steve then knew it was just a grad trick. His friends Neil and Shawn were laughing out of control behind a nearby bush.

(124 words)

RETELLING

Please retell the story.

COMPREHENSION

____ (I) How old do you think Steve was? Explain your answer. *(16, 17, 18 or 19 is acceptable, this is the age when students graduate from grade 12 or Steve was old enough to have a driver's license)*

____ (F) Why was Steve in a hurry? *(he was running late)*

____ (F) When did he hear the noise? *(as he pulled away from the curb)*

____ (F) What made the truck rock and roll? *(a rock was attached to the drive shaft)*

____ (I) How did Steve feel when he stopped the truck? *(angry; mad; frustrated; flustered; upset; annoyed – 1 out of 6)*

____ (F) What was used to attach the rock to the drive shaft? *(wire)*

____ (I) Who tied the rock to the drive shaft? *(Neil and Shawn; his two friends – 1 out of 2)*

READING LEVEL

Independent 6½ - 7 points	Instructional 4½ - 6 points	Frustration 4 points or less

PRIOR KNOWLEDGE

Have you ever had an experience with pranks before?

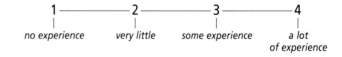

1 —————— 2 —————— 3 —————— 4

no experience   very little   some experience   a lot of experience

LEVEL OF INTEREST

How much did you like reading this story?

1 —————— 2 —————— 3 —————— 4

it was not interesting   it was fairly good   it was good   it was excellent

Student's Passage: page 46

Introduction: This is about the queen bee.

The Queen Bee

A bee colony is made up of three different types of bees. The biggest bee in a hive is the queen bee. The other bees are called drones and worker bees.

The male bees are the drones. Their purpose in life is to mate with the queen. The male bees take no part in the work of the hive. The queen bee is cared for by the worker bees.

The queen lays all the eggs in the colony. She only eats and lays eggs. She is fed a rich diet of royal jelly. The queen lays her eggs from January to November. The majority of eggs are laid between the first warm days of spring and the end of summer. Sometimes she lays 3,000 eggs per day.

When an old queen dies, a new queen emerges out of a cocoon. She then stabs all her sisters to death. There is only one queen bee in a hive.

(158 words)

RETELLING
Please retell the passage.

COMPREHENSION

____ (F) Name the three different types of bees.
(queen, worker bee, and drone)

____ (F) What is the drone's purpose in life? *(to mate with the queen)*

____ (F) What does the queen spend her time doing? Name two things. *(eating; mating; laying eggs - 2 out of 3)*

____ (I) Which bees do you think have the easiest job and which bees have the hardest job? *(drones have the easiest job and worker bees have the hardest job)*

____ (F) What does the queen bee eat? *(a rich diet of royal jelly)*

____ (I) Who do you think feeds the queen royal jelly? *(the worker bee)*

____ (F) When does the queen lay her eggs? *(from January to November; first warm days of spring and the end of summer – 1 out of 2)*

____ (I) What type of violence occurs in bee colonies? *(the new queen stabs all her sisters to death)*

READING LEVEL

Independent	Instructional	Frustration
7½ - 8 points	5½ - 7 points	5 points or less

PRIOR KNOWLEDGE
How much did you know about queen bees before you read this passage?

I knew:

1 ——————— 2 ——————— 3 ——————— 4
nothing   very little   something   a lot

LEVEL OF INTEREST
How much did you like reading this passage?

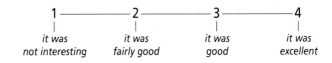

1 ——————— 2 ——————— 3 ——————— 4
it was   it was   it was   it was
not interesting fairly good   good   excellent

Introduction: This is about the life of a pioneer woman.

A Pioneer Woman

In old times a farm woman had to work hard. She often assisted her husband in the fields. She grew a vegetable garden for food. She looked after chickens and cattle. Or she made the children look after them.

A farm woman preserved food to eat in winter. She preserved meat and fish with salt. She dried berries and other foods. Every day she cooked the family meals.

It was difficult to keep the house clean. Dust and mud came into the house because there were no sidewalks outside. There were no vacuum cleaners. Someone had to sweep and scrub the floors.

If children were sick, the mother would nurse them. There were few doctors or hospitals in the country.

It was a lonely life for a woman. Most farms were far away from neighbors. The men were away working or hunting a lot of the time.

(147 words)

RETELLING

Please retell the passage.

COMPREHENSION

____ (F) List six chores of a woman who lived on a farm. *(assisting her husband in the fields; growing a garden; looking after chickens; looking after cattle; preserving food; drying berries; cooking the family meals; cleaning the house; nursing the children - 6 out of 9)*

____ (F) What kind of work did the children do? *(they looked after chickens and cattle)*

____ (I) Why would winter be an easier time of year for farm women? *(they would not have a garden to tend; they would not be preserving food; they would not be assisting their husbands in the field; they would not be cleaning outside dust and mud in the house; their husbands would be at home more – 1 out of 5)*

____ (F) Name three types of food they preserved for the winter season. *(meat, fish, and berries)*

____ (F) Tell three reasons why the houses were difficult to keep clean. *(there were no sidewalks; the dust and mud came into the house; there were no vacuums; they had to sweep and scrub the floors – 3 out of 4)*

____ (I) What do you think was the pioneer woman's most important job? Explain your answer. *(preserving food to eat in the winter because they would die without food; nursing children because there was little medical care – 1 out of 2)*

____ (F) Why did mothers nurse their sick children? *(there were few doctors or hospitals in the country)*

____ (I) Based on what you read in the passage, do you think a lot of children died? Explain your answer. *(yes, the mothers would not have the proper training and medicine to care for their children; yes, there were few doctors or hospitals – 1 out of 2)*

READING LEVEL

Independent	Instructional	Frustration
7½ - 8 points	5½ - 7 points	5 points or less

PRIOR KNOWLEDGE
How much did you know about the life of a pioneer woman before you read this passage?

I knew:

1	2	3	4
nothing	very little	something	a lot

LEVEL OF INTEREST
How much did you like reading this passage?

1	2	3	4
it was not interesting	it was fairly good	it was good	it was excellent

Student's Passage: page 48

Introduction: This is the story of a summer romance.

Summer Romance

Ann and Mike were students. They met one summer in an English class. Ann was from Spain. Mike was from Poland. They spent a lot of time with each other and fell in love. When the summer ended, Ann had to go back to Spain, and Mike had to go back to Poland. Before they parted, Mike promised to visit Ann in Spain.

Mike wrote to Ann every week. At first, Ann answered all his letters. Then Mike began to get fewer letters from Ann, but each letter from her was still full of love.

The next summer, Mike went to visit Ann in Spain. When he got there, he phoned her from the airport. Ann's sister answered the phone. She told Mike that Ann was married. Mike went back to Poland. He wrote Ann his last letter. It said: "You knew I was coming to visit. Why didn't you tell me you were married? I thought you loved me. I guess, for you, it was just a summer romance."

(170 words)

RETELLING
Please retell the story.

COMPREHENSION

____ (I) What language do you think Ann and Mike wrote letters to each other in? *(English)*

____ (I) What two things made this romance difficult? *(they lived far apart, and they communicated through letters)*

____ (F) What did Mike promise? *(to visit Ann in Spain)*

____ (F) How many letters did Mike write each week? *(one)*

____ (I) How do you think Mike felt when he learned Ann was married? *(shocked; sad; betrayed; unhappy; heartbroken; hurt; upset; disappointed – 1 out of 8)*

____ (F) When did Mike visit Ann? *(in the summer)*

____ (I) What word would you use to describe Mike? *(faithful; loyal; honest; nice; loving; romantic; sensitive; devoted; gullible; kind; caring - 1 out of 11)*

____ (I) How do you know that Mike never tried to contact Ann again? *(he wrote her his last letter; she got married - 1 out of 2)*

READING LEVEL

Independent	Instructional	Frustration
7½ - 8 points	5½ - 7 points	5 points or less

LEVEL OF INTEREST
How much did you like reading this story?

1	2	3	4
it was	*it was*	*it was*	*it was*
not interesting	*fairly good*	*good*	*excellent*

Student's Passage: page 49

Introduction: This is a story of a man learning a lesson.

The Piano Lesson

Joe saw an ad in the paper. It said, "Pianos for Sale – $199."

"What a deal!" thought Joe. "I can buy a piano for $199. I can sell it for ten times as much! This is too good to be true!" Joe sent the piano company a check.

Six weeks later, Joe got a small box in the mail. He opened the box. Inside, was a little plastic piano.

Joe got mad. He phoned the Better Business Bureau. The man on the phone asked Joe for the name and address of the piano company. The address was only a postbox number. The man checked his records. He told Joe that there was no record of the piano company.

Joe was sad. He had lost a lot of money on a little piano. But he did learn a big lesson – some things *are* too good to be true.

(147 words)

RETELLING
Please retell the story.

COMPREHENSION

____ (F) Why did Joe buy the piano? *(he thought he could sell it for ten times as much; he wanted to sell it – 1 out of 2)*

____ (F) How many weeks did it take for the piano to arrive? *(six)*

____ (I) What should have made Joe suspicious when he read the ad? *(there was no phone number or street address; there was no description of the piano; the price of the piano was too low – 1 out of 3)*

____ (I) What are two words you would use to describe the owners of the piano company? *(cons; crooks; dishonest; clever, liars, crafty; slick; fraudulent; swindlers - 2 out of 9)*

____ (I) What do you think Joe should have done before he purchased the piano? Name two things. *(phoned the piano company for more information; written the piano company for more information; phoned the Better Business Bureau; gone to see the piano - 2 out of 4)*

____ (I) Why do you think the piano company used a postbox number instead of a street address? *(the owners of the company didn't want people to find them)*

____ (F) How did Joe feel after he received the piano and found out there was no record of the piano company? Name two feelings. *(sad and mad)*

____ (F) Joe learned a big lesson. What was it? *(some things are too good to be true)*

READING LEVEL

Independent 7½ - 8 points	Instructional 5½ - 7 points	Frustration 5 points or less

LEVEL OF INTEREST
How much did you like reading this story?

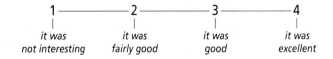

1	2	3	4
it was *not interesting*	*it was* *fairly good*	*it was* *good*	*it was* *excellent*

Student's Passage: page 50

Introduction: This is about hay fever.

Hay Fever

In the United States, about one in ten people suffers from hay fever. This condition causes sneezing, wheezing, and runny noses. It also makes the eyes red and swollen. The ears, nose, eyes, mouth, and skin may get itchy. Hay fever is often confused with the common cold.

Hay fever is an allergy to pollen. Some people are sensitive to tree pollen and snow mold. For these people, hay fever is worse in the spring. Others are sensitive to grass pollen. For these people, hay fever is worse during the summer. Some people suffer all year long. This is because they are allergic to dust mites and animal hair. Yeast, eggs, and milk have also been known to trigger hay fever.

There is no cure for hay fever. But, there are ways to control it. People should avoid pollens, molds, dust, and animals. Windows should be closed when pollen is in the air. People should also avoid going outdoors on hot, dry, windy days. They should spend time outside during the evening, rather than the day. This is when the pollen count is the lowest. To avoid dust, mattresses, box springs, and pillows should be cleaned. Then they should be covered with dust-proof covers.

There are a few ways to treat hay fever. People can buy tablets, nasal sprays, and eye drops. Some of these drugs need to be prescribed by a doctor. Others can be purchased over the counter. Finally, people can get allergy shots before hay fever season begins.

(253 words)

RETELLING
Please retell the passage.

COMPREHENSION

____ (F) In the United States, how many people suffer from hay sfever? *(one in ten)*

____ (I) Name three things that hay fever and the common cold have in common. *(sneezing; wheezing; runny noses; red eyes; swollen eyes – 3 out of 5)*

____ (F) In the spring, what are two things that trigger hay fever? *(tree pollen and snow mold)*

____ (I) Why do you think there are fewer cases of hay fever in the winter? *(there is no pollen)*

____ (F) What causes some people to suffer from hay fever all year long? *(dust mites; animal hair - 1 out of 2)*

____ (I) Why would bread trigger hay fever in some people? *(it contains yeast; it contains eggs; it contains milk - 1 out of 3)*

____ (F) Name three practical ways to avoid pollens, molds, and dust. *(close windows when pollen is in the air; avoid the outdoors on hot, dry, windy days; spend time outside during the evenings; clean mattresses, box springs and pillows; use dust-proof covers; stay inside; vacuum regularly; keep house clean - 3 out of 8)*

____ (I) What makes hay fever different from the common cold? *(hay fever is caused by allergies)*

____ (F) Name two household items that should be covered with a dust-proof cover. *(mattresses; box springs; pillows – 2 out of 3)*

____ (F) Name three ways to treat hay fever. *(tablets; nasal sprays; eye drops; allergy shots – 3 out of 4)*

READING LEVEL

Independent $9\frac{1}{2}$ - 10 points	Instructional 7 - 9 points	Frustration $6\frac{1}{2}$ points or less

PRIOR KNOWLEDGE
How much did you know about hay fever before reading this passage?

I knew:

1 — nothing   2 — very little   3 — something   4 — a lot

LEVEL OF INTEREST
How much did you like reading this passage?

1 — it was not interesting   2 — it was fairly good   3 — it was good   4 — it was excellent

Introduction: This is about beaver lodges.

Beaver Lodges

The beaver is the largest rodent in the United States. Beavers live in lodges located in lakes, rivers, ponds, and streams. Sometimes they construct dams in ponds and streams. The dams maintain a water supply to protect their lodges.

Beavers use their sharp teeth to gnaw through the trunks of young trees. Often, a newly felled tree will be a long way from the beaver's dam or lodge. If this happens, the beaver floats the log to the building site. Sometimes, it builds canals to let the log float freely. The beaver uses its front paws to put the trunks and branches into place.

The walls of the lodge are layers of logs held together with grass, debris, and mud. The roof, made of branches, is about three feet above the water level. A chimney is built into the roof to let air flow in and out of the lodge.

The entrance to the lodge is under water. The living room is above the water level. A tunnel connects the entrance to the living room. There is more than one exit from the lodge. This helps the beaver to escape if an enemy tries to enter.

Sometimes, many families live together in a colony. Each family builds and lives in its own lodge. An adult pair, newborn kits, and yearlings born the previous year occupy each lodge. Beavers spend most of their day building or fixing their lodge and dam.

(240 words)

RETELLING
Please retell the passage.

COMPREHENSION

____ (F) Name three places where beavers build lodges. *(in lakes; in rivers; in ponds; in streams – 3 out of 4)*

____ (F) Why do beavers sometimes construct dams? *(to maintain a water supply; to protect the beaver lodge - 1 out of 2)*

____ (F) What does a beaver do if a newly felled tree is a long way from its dam or lodge? *(it floats the log to the building site; builds canals to let the log float freely – 1 out of 2)*

____ (F) Name four materials that are used to build the lodge. *(logs; branches; grass; debris; mud; trees – 4 out of 6)*

____ (F) What is the purpose of the chimney? *(it lets air flow in and out of the lodge)*

____ (I) Name two parts of the lodge that are visible to the human eye. *(the roof; the chimney; the living room - 2 out of 3)*

____ (F) What is a colony? *(many families who live together)*

____ (F) Who occupies each lodge? *(an adult pair and kits and yearlings - ask "What else?" if the student only provides a partial response)*

____ (I) What is the difference between a kit and a yearling? *(a kit is younger; a yearling is older – 1 out of 2)*

____ (I) What word would you use to describe what the beaver is like? *(hardworking; industrious; busy; determined; protective – 1 out of 5)*

READING LEVEL

Independent $9\frac{1}{2}$ - 10 points	Instructional 7 - 9 points	Frustration $6\frac{1}{2}$ points or less

PRIOR KNOWLEDGE
How much did you know about beaver lodges before reading this passage?

I knew:

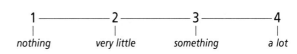

1 ———— 2 ———— 3 ———— 4
nothing   very little   something   a lot

LEVEL OF INTEREST
How much did you like reading this passage?

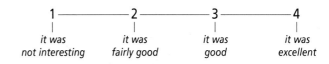

1 ———— 2 ———— 3 ———— 4
it was
not interesting   it was
fairly good   it was
good   it was
excellent

Introduction: This is a story about an unlucky bank robber.

The Unlucky Bank Robber

A heavyset man entered a bank and sat down in a chair in the reception area. He picked up a magazine and pretended to read it. After a couple of minutes, he lowered the magazine and surveyed his surroundings. He observed the security guards, noting that there were two of them and they both had guns. His gaze turned towards the bank tellers behind the shiny, protective glass. Then, he happened to glance up at the vaulted ceiling. He saw a skylight – and smiled. He put down the magazine and went home.

The man waited for the sun to set, and then he returned to the bank. He climbed on to the roof and cautiously stepped over to the skylight. He shattered the glass with a big rock and waited. No alarm. The man started to lower himself through the skylight when suddenly he got stuck. He attempted to escape, but the skylight was too small.

The next morning, the janitor arrived to clean the bank. "Oh my gosh!" he cried. He called the police. "There are two legs sticking out of the ceiling," he told them.

The police arrived in ten minutes and helped the poor robber get through the skylight. Then they escorted him to jail.

(208 words)

RETELLING
Please retell the story.

COMPREHENSION

____ (F) What were the first two things the man did when he entered the bank? *(sat down in a chair and picked up a magazine)*

____ (F) Name three things the bank robber noticed when he surveyed his surroundings. *(two security guards; guards; bank tellers behind shiny, protective glass; skylight; vaulted ceiling; both guards had guns – 3 out of 6)*

____ (I) Name two kinds of protection that the bank provided for the bank tellers. *(protective glass and security guards)*

____ (I) What was the bank robber waiting for after he broke the glass in the skylight? *(an alarm)*

____ (I) Why do you think the alarm didn't go off? *(because the robber entered through a sky light rather than a door; skylight was not connected to the alarm system – 1 out of 2)*

____ (I) How do you know that the bank robber did not have much experience in robbing banks? *(he did not take much time to plan the robbery; the robbery was not well planned; he got caught; skylight was a poor choice for entering the bank – 1 out of 4)*

____ (F) What did the janitor see when he arrived at the bank? *(two legs sticking out of the ceiling)*

____ (I) Approximately how many hours was the bank robber stuck in the skylight? *(accept anything from 7 hours to 15 hours)*

READING LEVEL

Independent	Instructional	Frustration
7½ - 8 points	5½ - 7 points	5 points or less

LEVEL OF INTEREST
How much did you like reading this story?

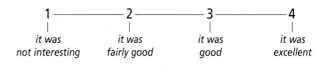

1 —————— 2 —————— 3 —————— 4
| | | |
it was   *it was*   *it was*   *it was*
not interesting   *fairly good*   *good*   *excellent*

Introduction: This story is about a mysterious figure who is watching a woman.

Silent Watcher

Ken kissed her good night at the front entry of the apartment block. Noreen walked down the hallway to Number 7 and unlocked her door. Stepping inside, she flicked on the light and hurried to the patio doors. She pulled back the sheers and peered out to the street. Ken was waiting for her signal before heading home himself.

He returned Noreen's wave and disappeared down the street. As she turned away from the window, a chill crept through her that had nothing to do with the March night. She saw what looked to be a person hiding behind the shrubs near the end of her building. Her heart beat faster as she ran back to the light switch. With the room darker now, Noreen again went to the patio doors to get a better look outside. Yes, there he was, almost hidden by the branches. He had on a winter hat of some sort and a scarf, from what she could make out.

Noreen began to pace, trying not to worry. After half an hour, she checked outside again. The figure was still at his post, not moving, just watching. She phoned Ken, who had just got home. "I'm scared, Ken, he's just standing there, watching my apartment!"

When Ken heard the rest of the details, he started to laugh. "The sun will look after your peeping Tom tomorrow, honey," he said. "I saw that guy as I left your place. It's a snowman!"

(244 words)

RETELLING
Please retell the story.

COMPREHENSION

____ (F) Where did Noreen live? *(in suite 7; in an apartment block – 1 out of 2)*

____ (F) What was Ken waiting for before he headed home? *(a signal; a wave - 1 out of 2)*

____ (I) Why did a chill creep through Noreen? *(she thought someone was hiding; she thought someone was watching her – 1 out of 2)*

____ (F) Where was the peeping Tom? *(behind the shrubs; near the end of her building – 1 out of 2)*

____ (I) What word would you use to describe Noreen's personality? *(cautious; a worrier; nervous – 1 out of 3 (do not accept scared as this is how she felt))*

____ (I) How long did it take Ken to get home? *(accept anything between 30 to 35 minutes)*

____ (I) When Noreen phoned Ken, what do you think she wanted him to do? *(return to her apartment; protect her; find out who was watching her – 1 out of 3)*

____ (I) What was Ken and Noreen's relationship? *(they were more than just friends; they were dating each other; they were boyfriend and girlfriend – 1 out of 3)*

READING LEVEL

Independent	Instructional	Frustration
$7\frac{1}{2}$ - 8 points	$5\frac{1}{2}$ - 7 points	5 points or less

LEVEL OF INTEREST
How much did you like reading this story?

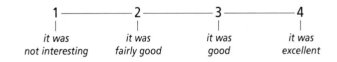

1	2	3	4
it was not interesting	*it was fairly good*	*it was good*	*it was excellent*

Introduction: This is about how supermarkets display their products so that you buy more.

Supermarket Temptations

Do you ever go to the food store for a quart of milk and then end up leaving with a bag of groceries? Food stores are designed to tempt you to buy groceries. Careful shoppers know how to avoid being tempted by items they don't really need.

In most stores, the milk is located as far from the door as possible. That is because most shoppers buy milk. So the store owners want to make sure you have to walk past a lot of merchandise on your way to the dairy case. Along that route you'll also find snacks and baked goods. These are items that people are most likely to buy on impulse.

The ends of aisles are speed bumps. As you slow down to go around them, you may spot a stack of paper towels. Since they are out of their usual place, you may think they are on sale. Again, this is another way that store owners entice you to buy their products.

Giving in to temptation is hard on a budget. So it is important to learn ways to leave the store with your budget intact. Plan your weekly meals and then make up a grocery list. As you look for the items on the list, remember to be flexible. For example, if you've planned on buying cod for dinner, but it costs too much, opt for sole. Also, make a mental list of the standard prices of your usual purchases. By doing this, you will know a bargain when you see one. Finally, use coupons only for the items on your list. You aren't saving money if you use the coupons on foods you don't need in the first place. (284 words)

RETELLING
Please retell the passage.

COMPREHENSION

____ (F) What are food stores designed for? *(to tempt you to buy groceries)*

____ (I) Why is the end of an aisle called a speed bump? *(you have to slow down to go around the aisle)*

____ (F) According to the author, what are two kinds of food that people buy on impulse? *(snacks and baked goods)*

____ (F) What do you think if a food item is out of its usual place? *(that it is on sale)*

____ (F) According to the author, what is one way store owners entice you to buy their products? *(products are placed on the ends of aisles; products are placed in areas where you have to slow down and then you look at them; impulse items are placed in areas that you need to pass on your way to the dairy case - 1 out of 3)*

____ (I) Peanut butter is always located beside jam and jelly. What do you think you should do if you see a display of peanut butter at the front of the store? *(check the price to see if it is on sale)*

____ (F) Name three things you can do to leave the store with your budget intact. *(plan weekly meals and then make up a grocery list; be flexible; know your prices, use coupons for items on the list – 3 out of 4)*

____ (F) What did the author say you should remember to be as you look for items on your grocery list? *(flexible)*

____ (I) Let's say you go to the store to buy fish, rice, lettuce, and tomatoes. In the store, the clerk gives you a coupon for $1.00 off egg rolls. What should you do if you are on a budget? *(don't use the coupon)*

____ (I) Explain how coupons can be a waste of money. *(you might buy food that you normally wouldn't buy)*

READING LEVEL

Independent	Instructional	Frustration
9½ - 10 points	7 - 9 points	6½ points or less

PRIOR KNOWLEDGE
How much did you know about the design of supermarkets before reading this passage?

I knew:

1 ——— 2 ——— 3 ——— 4

nothing   very little   something   a lot

LEVEL OF INTEREST
How much did you like reading this passage?

1 ——— 2 ——— 3 ——— 4

it was   it was   it was   it was
not interesting   fairly good   good   excellent

Introduction: This is about goalies.

Goalies

Hockey goalies have made a special place for themselves in sports. They are often called loners, or at least they prefer to be alone before, during, and after a game. They have superstitions. Some will talk only to certain players before a game, while others will let only some players tap their goal pads with a stick. Glenn Hall played over 500 consecutive games in his career and threw up before each one. Patrick Roy talks to his goal posts and steps over each line on the ice while skating to and from his net.

In the old days, goalies could not go down to stop a shot. They never wore masks, and they had no back-ups. If one of them was cut, the team doctor would stitch him up and put him back in the net. Once, in the Stanley Cup final, New York Rangers coach Lester Patrick had to play goal when his goalie could not return to the game. The Rangers won the cup.

Jacques Plante was the first goalie to wear a mask in a game. Consequently, he was called a sissy. His face had been cut, and his team still needed him, so he pulled out a mask and put it on.

Today, all goalies wear masks, but they still have plenty to be worried about. Players can shoot the puck over 60 miles per hour. The game is faster. Plus, goalies have additional responsibilities. They handle the puck now and make passes to clear the zone. They have even scored the odd goal.

(260 words)

RETELLING
Please retell the passage.

COMPREHENSION

____ (F) Name one way that goalies have made a special place for themselves in sports. *(they are loners; they are superstitious – 1 out of 2)*

____ (F) Name two common superstitions among goalies. *(some will talk only to certain players before a game and others will let only some players tap their goal pads with a stick)*

____ (I) Do you think that a goalie would go out with his team mates after a game? Explain your answer. *(no, they are loners)*

____ (I) What almost prevented the New York Rangers from winning the Stanley Cup? *(the coach was acting as the goalie; the goalie could not finish the game – 1 out of 2)*

____ (I) In the old days, why was it difficult for goalies to prevent the other team from scoring a goal? *(they could not go down to stop a shot)*

____ (F) In the old days, what would happen if a goalie was cut? *(the team doctor would stitch him up and put him back in the net)*

____ (F) Who was the first goalie to wear a mask in a game? *(Jacques Plante)*

____ (F) Why did Jacques Plante put on a mask? *(his face was cut, and his team still needed him)*

____ (F) Today, goalies have additional responsibilities. Name two of them. *(handling the puck and making passes to clear the zone)*

____ (I) Why is being a goalie dangerous today? *(the game is faster; a puck can travel up to 60 miles per hour; a goalie could get injured by the puck – 1 out of 3)*

READING LEVEL

Independent	Instructional	Frustration
$9\frac{1}{2}$ - 10 points	7 - 9 points	$6\frac{1}{2}$ points or less

PRIOR KNOWLEDGE

How much did you know about goalies before reading this passage?

I knew:

1 ——————— 2 ——————— 3 ——————— 4
nothing   very little   something   a lot

LEVEL OF INTEREST

How much did you like reading this passage?

1 ——————— 2 ——————— 3 ——————— 4
it was   it was   it was   it was
not interesting fairly good   good   excellent

Introduction: This is a story about a man's fight to survive.

Fire and a Friend

Howard crawled out of bed, quickly pulling on his blue jeans and ski jacket. Bare feet slid into chilly boots. Growling at the 6:05 a.m. clock face, he grabbed some matches from the dresser and shuffled to the furnace room.

The pilot light was out again. He crouched by the furnace and lit the match. The explosion threw him against the cement wall. Angry flames surrounded him, but his ears were deaf to their roar. His nose and throat burned with smoke and heat as he tried to breathe. Everything was out of place. Howard was alone and trapped!

Howard blindly fought through the blaze. Finally reaching the outdoors, he gratefully threw himself into the coolness of the snow.

The injured man squinted toward the lights of a house just across the railway tracks. Ed would be having his morning coffee. As Howard stumbled to the crossing, he saw with horror that a train blocked his path.

"If I crawl under it, it may start moving and run over me," Howard spoke to himself. "I'll have to climb between the cars."

His body painfully worked over the iron connection. The skin from the palms of his hands stayed on the cold metal joint. Wheezing at the door of Ed's house, Howard kicked it with a charred boot.

Ed saw a shape that didn't even look human, whispering, "Help!" The stranger's face was a puffy mask. His hair and parts of his ears were burned off. His jacket was a collar with a zipper, and two wrist bands above blistered hands.

As Ed drove the suffering man to the hospital, he wondered if this brave stranger would live. Ed didn't know he had just saved his friend's life.

(289 words)

RETELLING
Please retell the story.

COMPREHENSION

____ (F) What did Howard do when he got out of bed? *(checked the time; put on clothes; grabbed some matches; went to the furnace room; lit the pilot light – 4 out of 5 – ask "What else?" if the student only provides three responses)*

____ (I) What kind of mood was Howard in when he went to the furnace room? *(angry; mad; grumpy; grouchy; bad mood; unhappy - 1 out of 6)*

____ (I) How do you know that Howard didn't want to get out of bed in the morning? *(he crawled out of bed; he growled at the clock face; it was 6:05 – 1 out of 3)*

____ (F) Name three things that Howard was wearing when he went down to the furnace room. *(boots, ski jacket and jeans)*

____ (I) Was this the first time that Howard had experienced difficulty with his furnace? Explain your answer. *(no, the pilot light had gone out before)*

____ (I) People have five senses. Which two senses did Howard lose as he fought his way through the blaze? (hearing; seeing; smell – 2 out of 3)

____ (I) Describe Howard's character. *(determined; had good judgment; brave; courageous; a fighter; optimistic - 1 out of 6)*

____ (F) What did Howard decide to do when he saw a train blocking his path? *(climb between the cars)*

____ (F) Describe Howard's appearance when he reached Ed's house. Provide four descriptions. *(face a puffy mask; his hair burnt off; parts of ears burnt off; hands blistered; jacket a collar with a zipper and two wrist bands; didn't look human – 4 out of 6)*

____ (I) Do you think Howard and Ed talked during the car ride to the hospital? Explain your answer. *(no, because Ed thought Howard was a stranger; no, Howard was in too much pain to talk; yes, Ed wanted to comfort Howard – 1 out of 3)*

READING LEVEL

Independent	Instructional	Frustration
$9\frac{1}{2}$ - 10 points	7 - 9 points	$6\frac{1}{2}$ points or less

LEVEL OF INTEREST

How much did you like reading this story?

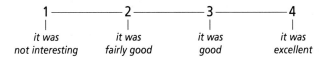

1 — 2 — 3 — 4

it was — it was — it was — it was
not interesting — fairly good — good — excellent

Introduction: This is the story about a key witness's confession to the FBI.

The Star Witness

The FBI agent burst into the chief's office.

"We've got them! Baker, Maffie, Pino – the whole stinking lot. O'Keefe confessed everything. I cannot believe how good these crooks were. They were casing the building, making plans, walking in and out of that place for two years. They knew everything – security systems, schedules, who turned what light on when. You want to know how they got inside?"

The agent flipped through his tattered notebook.

"There it is. They removed the door locks, replaced them with bogus locks, and brought the locks to some locksmith on the other side of Boston. He made keys for the locks, and once they had the keys, they went back into the building and replaced the bogus locks with the original locks. Nobody suspected. These guys were crawling around the place for two years, and nobody suspected a thing! The Brinks building, for God's sakes! It's the safest building in Boston."

"Why confess now, after six years?" asked the chief.

"O'Keefe feels the other gang members ripped him off," said the agent. "He never got his money. They unloaded pieces of the get-away truck in a dump near his house. He feels he's on his own. He said – and I quote – they all agreed that if anyone messed up, they would be 'taken care of.' O'Keefe figures they messed up. Talking to us is his way of taking care of them."

The Chief sighed, then smiled. "Let's finish this," he said. (246 words)

RETELLING
Please retell the story.

COMPREHENSION

____ (I) Who was the star witness? *(O'Keefe)*

____ (I) What type of crime was committed? *(robbery; break and entry – 1 out of 2)*

____ (F) Who investigated the crime? *(the FBI)*

____ (I) How many people were involved in planning the robbery? *(four)*

____ (F) Name three types of information the gang members gathered in the two years prior to the robbery? *(security system; schedules; who turned the different lights on; layout of the building – 3 out of 4)*

____ (F) Name two ways in which O'Keefe was ripped off by the other gang members. *(they dumped parts of the get-away truck in a dump near his house and they didn't give him his share of the money)*

____ (I) How did O'Keefe seek revenge? *(he talked to the FBI; he confessed – 1 out of 2)*

____ (F) How many years did it take for O'Keefe to confess? *(six)*

____ (I) Why do you think it took so long for O'Keefe to confess? *(he probably thought that if he confessed, he would be "taken care of" ; he thought he would be killed; he was still waiting for his share of the money - 1 out of 3)*

____ (I) In this story, what do the words "taken care of" mean? *(you will be hurt; you will be killed; you will be betrayed; you will be punished - 1 out of 4)*

READING LEVEL

Independent	Instructional	Frustration
$9\frac{1}{2}$ - 10 points	7 - 9 points	$6\frac{1}{2}$ points or less

LEVEL OF INTEREST
How much did you like reading this story?

1	2	3	4
it was not interesting	it was fairly good	it was good	it was excellent

Introduction: This is about high blood pressure.

High Blood Pressure

High blood pressure increases the risk of heart disease and stroke. The "silent killer" is a name given to high blood pressure. This is because people who have it do not feel sick. A person may suffer from the condition for years without feeling any different at all. So people need to have their blood pressure checked each year by a doctor.

Blood pressure that is 140/90 or above is high. The first number, 140, is the force of the blood in the arteries when the heart is pumping blood out. The second number, 90, is the force of the blood in the arteries when the heart is filling with blood. Blood pressure varies with the time of day, activity, and stress. So it should be measured at least three times to make sure that the result is accurate.

Women and men are at special risk for developing high blood pressure if they come from families with a history of this condition. There are also certain times in a woman's life that may cause high blood pressure. Pregnant women can experience this condition in the last three months before delivery. Also, after menopause, women are more likely to suffer from high blood pressure than are men the same age.

There are some warning signs that indicate high blood pressure. A person may feel tired and dizzy. As well, a person may get headaches and a lot of nosebleeds. Other symptoms include a ringing in the ears and a flushed face.

High blood pressure can be prevented or controlled in a number of ways. People should use less salt in cooking and at the table. Instead, food should be seasoned with herbs and spices. Eating garlic can also help to reduce blood pressure. People should avoid smoking and limit their use of alcohol. Lastly, exercise such as walking or biking has been known to bring high blood pressure down to normal. Exercise will also assist weight loss. This, in turn, will lower blood pressure. If these methods do not work, drugs might be needed.

(344 words)

RETELLING
Please retell the passage.

COMPREHENSION

_____ (F) What is a name given to high blood pressure? *(the silent killer)*

_____ (I) Why can heart disease and stroke seem to occur without warning? *(heart disease and stroke may be caused by high blood pressure, and people suffering from high blood pressure may not feel sick)*

_____ (F) How many times should blood pressure be measured in order to ensure accurate results? *(three times)*

_____ (I) Would a blood pressure of 110/80 be considered low, average, or high? *(average)*

_____ (F) Let's say your blood pressure is 140/90. What is the meaning of the first number? *(the force of the blood in the arteries when the heart is pumping blood out)*

_____ (F) What causes a person's blood pressure to vary? *(time of day; activity; stress – 1 out of 3)*

_____ (I) Name two important times for women to check their blood pressure. *(during the last three months of pregnancy and after menopause)*

_____ (I) Why do you think some athletes have high blood pressure? *(they come from families with a history of this condition; they drink too much; they eat a lot of salt; they are under a lot of stress – 1 out of 4)*

_____ (F) Name four warning signs of high blood pressure. *(tiredness; dizziness; headaches; nosebleeds; ringing in the ears; flushed face – 4 out of 6)*

_____ (F) Name two ways to control high blood pressure through cooking and eating. *(use less salt in cooking; use less salt at the table; eat garlic; eat less if you are overweight; season foods with herbs and spices – 2 out of 5)*

READING LEVEL

Independent	Instructional	Frustration
$9\frac{1}{2}$ points	7 - 9 points	$6\frac{1}{2}$ points or less

PRIOR KNOWLEDGE
How much did you know about high blood pressure before reading this passage?
I knew:

1 — nothing 2 — very little 3 — something 4 — a lot

LEVEL OF INTEREST
How much did you like reading this passage?

1 — it was not interesting 2 — it was fairly good 3 — it was good 4 — it was excellent

Introduction: This is about the Jewish celebration called Hanukkah.

Hanukkah

Hanukkah is a Jewish holiday that lasts for eight days during December. Jews celebrate a victory that took place more than 2000 years ago. A foreign power ruled the country. The temple was in the hands of the foreign army. It was the most holy place of the Jews and the center of their religion. Judah the Maccabee led a small group of Jews. They opposed the Greek armies and recaptured the temple.

The Jews felt that the temple had been defiled by the foreigners. It had to be cleaned and purified with rituals. It had to be dedicated to the service of God again. They went to relight the holy lamp in the temple, but there was only a small jar that held enough oil for one day. However, a miracle kept the lamp alight for eight days. These eight days marked the first Hanukkah celebration.

Hanukkah is called the Festival of the Lights. A menorah, which holds eight candles plus a "helper" candle, is lit every night. The eight candles stand for the eight days of Hanukkah. On the first night, the head of the family uses the helper candle to light one of the candles. Every evening, one more candle is lit. The candles burn for about half an hour. While they are burning, no one is supposed to do any work. After the lighting of the candles, there are special prayers to recall the brave Hebrews who fought to recover their country and the temple.

Some children receive money, which is called "Hanukkah Gelt," on the first day of the holiday. Other children get chocolate coins wrapped in gold foil. Small gifts are also exchanged during the holiday. The children play with a wooden spinning top that is called a driedl. The four sides of the top are marked with four Hebrew letters that stand for the words "A great miracle happened there."

All families eat special foods, such as latkes, during the Hanukkah celebration. Latkes are potato pancakes fried in oil.

(336 words)

RETELLING
Please retell the passage.

COMPREHENSION

____ (F) Why was the temple important to the Jewish people? *(it was their most holy place; it was the center of their religion – 1 out of 2)*

____ (I) During what month did the Jewish people defeat the Greek armies? *(December)*

____ (F) When did the first Hanukkah take place? *(more than 2000 years ago)*

____ (F) What was the miracle that occurred in the temple? *(there was only enough oil to light the lamp for one day and a miracle kept the lamp alight for eight days)*

____ (I) Why is Hanukkah called the Festival of the Lights? *(because of the miracle; because candles on the menorah are lit – 1 out of 2)*

____ (F) What does the family do after the menorah is lit? *(the family prays)*

____ (F) When are people supposed to stop working during Hanukkah? *(when the candles are burning)*

____ (I) On which evening does the menorah provide the most light? *(the eighth evening; the last evening – 1 out of 2)*

____ (F) What is a driedl? *(a wooden top; a spinning top; a top. **If the student says "toy", ask them to describe it** – 1 out of 3)*

____ (F) Name two things that children receive on the first day of the holiday. *(money and chocolate coins)*

READING LEVEL

Independent	Instructional	Frustration
$9\frac{1}{2}$ - 10 points	7 - 9 points	$6\frac{1}{2}$ points or less

PRIOR KNOWLEDGE
How much did you know about Hanukkah before reading this passage?

I knew:

1	2	3	4
nothing	very little	something	a lot

LEVEL OF INTEREST
How much did you like reading this passage?

1	2	3	4
it was not interesting	it was fairly good	it was good	it was excellent

Student's Passage: page 60

Introduction: This is a story about a midnight intruder.

Midnight Intruder

A number of break-ins had occurred in the Milton's neighborhood. With her husband away on business, Susan was afraid for her young son and herself. After the late news on TV that night, she locked all the doors and windows and made sure the timer light was set. For her own peace of mind, a baseball bat stood near her bed.

The next morning, Susan awoke to sun shining through her bedroom window and a squirming toddler attempting to get under the covers. She scooped Tommy up with a kiss and marched to the kitchen for breakfast. As she turned to the stove, the smile faded and her mouth went dry. The wooden lid of the glass cookie jar lay silently on the counter. How had that happened? Tommy was too small to reach that high, and there were no telltale crumbs on his fuzzy pajamas.

That night Susan took a long time to fall asleep, but at 1:30 a.m. her eyes flew open as she held her breath and listened closely. Someone was rattling the elements on the stove! Hearing a scraping noise at the sink, she grabbed the bat and tiptoed to the kitchen. A floorboard creaked beneath her just as she lunged through the doorway with the bat poised above her, ready to strike the intruder. The night light dimly lit an empty kitchen, the cookie jar lid on the counter, and a knife in the sink. Susan was trembling with fear and relief.

Wednesday night Susan was ready for the prowler, with her movie camera set to film the counter between the stove and sink. Drifting off to sleep, she heard it again – someone was in the kitchen! Half an hour passed as she tightly gripped the bat and prayed the intruder would leave. When Susan was sure there were no more sounds from the kitchen, she crept out to view the crime video.

Captured on tape, the culprit turned out to be a mouse, with the amazing ability to work the lid off the cookie jar whenever he pleased!

(347 words)

RETELLING
Please retell the story.

COMPREHENSION

____ (F) Why was Susan afraid? *(her husband was away; there had been a number of break-ins; she was alone with her son – 1 out of 3)*

____ (F) Name two ways Susan secured the house before she went to bed. *(locked all the doors and windows and made sure the timer light was set)*

____ (F) What did Susan do for her own peace of mind when she went to bed? *(put a baseball bat near her bed)*

____ (I) How many years old was Tommy? *(1 year old; 2 years old; 3 years – 1 out of 3)*

____ (I) How did she feel when she discovered the lid off the cookie jar? *(frightened; scared; nervous; puzzled; afraid – 1 out of 5)*

____ (F) One night, Susan woke up at 1:30. What did she hear? *(someone rattling the elements on the stove; a scraping noise at the sink; someone in the kitchen – 1 out of 3)*

____ (I) How do you think Susan treated her son? *(she was loving; she was protective; she took good care of him – 1 out of 3)*

____ (I) What do you think Susan did once she knew the intruder was a mouse? *(set mouse traps; laughed - 1 out of 2)*

____ (I) What word would you use to describe the kind of person Susan was? *(determined; creative; careful; alert; cautious; protective; persistent; brave; curious; courageous - 1 out of 10)*

____ (I) In your opinion, how can you tell that Susan was an independent woman? *(she didn't ask for help when she was afraid; she solved the mystery of the midnight intruder by herself - 1 out of 2 – **if the student says "It didn't say in the passage" – ask "What do you think?")***

READING LEVEL

Independent	Instructional	Frustration
$9\frac{1}{2}$ - 10 points	7 - 9 points	$6\frac{1}{2}$ points or less

LEVEL OF INTEREST
How much did you like reading this story?

1————————2————————3————————4

it was not interesting	it was fairly good	it was good	it was excellent

Introduction: This is the story of a woman's yearly visit to a special hotel.

Greta's Vigil

Greta paid for the hotel room. She carried her luggage to the second floor corner room, just as she had done for 28 years. The room was a bit more expensive now. Each year, the price went up a little, and the quality of the hotel lessened. But she expected that. The years had not been kind to her either.

When she was a bride those many years ago, her groom had gently lifted her and carried her over the threshold of Number 3 suite. Greta closed her eyes and hugged her body, recalling how her arms and his fit perfectly around each other, and how much the couple was in love. How she longed now to feel his embrace. There was a wonderful scent about Philip, she recalled. Was she dreaming, or did she smell that sweet odor right now?

That bright, starlit night in May lived in Greta's memory as clearly as if it had been just yesterday. Many gray hairs and unwanted wrinkles had appeared since then. She hoped Philip would still find her attractive. From her suitcase, she produced a framed snapshot of a smiling wedding couple. Yes, she had changed quite a lot since that photo was taken. She laid out her lacy nightgown on the tattered bedspread. She carefully placed a red rose upon the pillow as she turned back the covers. Greta heard her lover say, "We need champagne! I'll be right back, darling. This is to be a special evening. By the way, did I mention I love you more than life itself?" She felt a gentle kiss brush her lips, and he was gone – just as it had been 28 years ago.

Greta waited for his return, as she did on each anniversary of her wedding and of her husband's death. (300 words)

RETELLING
Please retell the story.

COMPREHENSION

____ (F) What was Greta waiting for? *(the return of her husband)*

____ (F) Name two ways the hotel had changed since Greta's first stay. *(the hotel prices had gone up a little, and the quality of the hotel had been lowered)*

____ (I) How many times a year did Greta return to the hotel? *(once a year)*

____ (F) What did Greta remember about their last night together? Name four things. *(being carried over the threshold; how their arms fit perfectly around each other; how much they were in love; Philip's scent; Philip's sweet odor; the bright starlit night; Philip's gentle kiss; Philip's last words; that he went to get champagne – 4 out of 9)*

____ (I) During what season did Greta and Philip marry? *(spring, ask "what season" if the student says "May")*

____ (I) How old do you think Greta is? *(any answer that indicates that she is in her late 40s or older is acceptable)*

____ (F) Name three things that Greta brought with her to the hotel room. *(rose; wedding photo; lacy nightgown; suitcase – 3 out of 4)*

____ (I) On what night did Philip die? *(on his honeymoon; on his wedding night; a night in May – 1 out of 3)*

____ (F) Before his death, what did Philip want to buy? *(champagne)*

____ (I) How many years had Greta been a widow? *(28 years)*

READING LEVEL

Independent $9\frac{1}{2}$ - 10 points	Instructional 7 - 9 points	Frustration $6\frac{1}{2}$ points or less

LEVEL OF INTEREST
How much did you like reading this story?

1	2	3	4
it was not interesting	it was fairly good	it was good	it was excellent

Introduction: This is about food poisoning.

Food Poisoning

In the United States, there are over 14 million cases of food poisoning each year. This condition is caused by germs. Salmonella is a common germ found in meat, poultry, eggs, and egg products. The symptoms of salmonella food poisoning include nausea, stomach cramps, diarrhea, fever, and headache. These symptoms usually occur 6 to 72 hours after eating the food and can last from 3 to 5 days.

Food poisoning is caused by a chain of events. First, there must be germs, such as salmonella or E. coli, on the food. These germs need the right conditions to grow: warmth, moisture, and food. The germs grow best in a moist setting where the temperature ranges between 41 to 140 degrees Fahrenheit. The germs also need a food source, such as dairy and egg products, meat, poultry, or fish, in order to grow and multiply. In ideal conditions, one germ can multiply to 2,097,152 within 7 hours.

The best defense against food poisoning is to take the offensive – to work actively to prevent it. Cooked or refrigerated foods, such as potato salad, should not sit at room temperature for more than two hours. The last items that shoppers should pick up are frozen foods, along with those that can perish. These items should be placed in the fridge and freezer as soon as possible. As the temperature of food goes down, so does the risk of organisms growing in it.

Heat kills most germs, even the hardy E.coli. But, for this to happen, all parts of the food must reach 158 degrees Fahrenheit. If microwaves are used, it is important to turn the food several times so that it is evenly heated. Food such as eggs, meat, and fish should never be eaten raw. For instance, raw eggs should not be used in Caesar salads or eggnog.

Food is contaminated through poor handling and lack of personal hygiene by those who prepare and serve it. It is important to wash hands with soap and warm water before food is prepared and after using the bathroom. During food preparation, hands, knives, and equipment such as cutting boards can become infected with germs from raw food such as meat. If the same equipment and knives are used to prepare another dish, such as carrots, the second dish can become infected with germs from the raw food. If the carrots are not cooked again before being eaten, the germs will not be killed. So it is a good idea to use separate cutting boards for meats and vegetables. From time to time, cutting boards should be soaked in bleach. By following these simple guidelines, one can avoid food poisoning.

(448 words)

RETELLING
Please retell the passage.

COMPREHENSION

_____ (F) How many cases of food poisoning occur each year in the United States? *(over 14 million)*

_____ (F) Name four types of food where salmonella grows. *(dairy products; egg products; meat; poultry; fish – 4 out of 5)*

_____ (F) Name four symptoms of salmonella food poisoning. *(nausea; stomach cramps; diarrhea; fever; headache – 4 out of 5)*

_____ (I) Let's say you went out for dinner and ate a rare steak. Four days later you get stomach cramps and diarrhea. Do you think you would have food poisoning? Explain your answer. *(no, food poisoning occurs within 72 hours)*

_____ (F) Name three conditions that germs need in order to grow. *(warmth, moisture, and food)*

_____ (F) What are the last two items you should purchase when you shop? *(frozen foods and perishables)*

_____ (I) From what you've read, what do you think is the best kind of sandwich to take in a brown paper bag for lunch? *(accept any answer that does not contain a filling with eggs, dairy products, meat, chicken, or fish)*

_____ (I) Why do you think it is dangerous to take potato salad on a picnic? *(it will be sitting at room temperature for more than 2 hours, and germs will grow in it; it will become warm, and germs will grow in it – 1 out of 2)*

_____ (I) Ideally, how many cutting boards should you be using when you prepare meals? Explain your answer. *(two, one for vegetables and one for meat and fish)*

_____ (F) Name three guidelines you should follow to avoid food poisoning when you are cooking. *(wash hands with soap and warm water before food is prepared; wash hands after using the bathroom; use different cutting boards and knives for vegetables and meats; soak cutting boards in bleach; do not let food sit out for more than 2 hours; food should reach 158 degrees Fahrenheit when it is cooked – 3 out of 6)*

READING LEVEL

Independent 9½ - 10 points	Instructional 7 - 9 points	Frustration 6½ points or less

PRIOR KNOWLEDGE

How much did you know about food poisoning before reading this passage?

I knew:

1 —————— 2 —————— 3 —————— 4

nothing   very little   something   a lot

LEVEL OF INTEREST

How much did you like reading this passage?

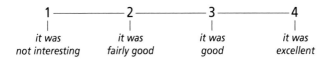

1 —————— 2 —————— 3 —————— 4

it was   it was   it was   it was
not interesting   fairly good   good   excellent

Introduction: This is about the construction of the railroad in British Columbia.

Finishing the Railroad

British Columbia became part of Canada in 1871. Before that, it was a colony of Britain. The mountains created a barrier between the West Coast and the rest of the country, restricting the travel and trade between them. It was easier for people on the coast to trade with the United States, as most river valleys lay south and north between ranges of mountains. As well, travel along the coast by ship was much faster than travelling overland to the East.

American people living on the West Coast had much in common with British Columbians: mining, logging, ocean products, and shipping were important to both. The Americans wanted the colony and wanted B.C. to join the United States. The Prime Minister of Canada dreamed of a "vast dominion" stretching from sea to sea that included B.C. He promised the people of the West Coast a railroad to connect B.C. to the rest of Canada, assuring them it would be finished within ten years. British Columbia agreed to enter into Confederation on the condition that railway construction would commence in two years and be completed in ten.

The railway was a very expensive and daunting project. A train can move uphill on a shallow grade, but it cannot pull itself up mountains. Sometimes the railway had to go through the rock instead of around it. In certain places, whole pieces of mountain were blasted out of the way by explosives. The flying pieces of rock sometimes caused landslides or killed workers. The railway had to follow river valleys as much as possible. Many men drowned while building bridges over swift rivers. Six hundred trestles and bridges were constructed, and 27 tunnels were blasted through solid rock.

It was almost impossible to recruit enough workers to do this strenuous, perilous work. The railway company brought almost 9000 men via ship from China to construct the section of track through the mountains. These men came seeking to make a lot of money, yet they were paid less than the other workers. Some hoped to acquire land and remain in Canada. The Chinese workers often performed the hardest and most hazardous tasks. Before the railway was completed, over 600 had died in explosions and other accidents.

In 1885 the railroad joining British Columbia to the rest of the country was completed. Few Chinese men remained in Canada because the government refused to let Chinese women or their families enter the country. Moreover, the workers were not welcome to stay. It was an unfortunate chapter in Canadian history.

(426 words)

RETELLING
Please retell the passage.

COMPREHENSION

____ (F) In what year did British Columbia become part of Canada? *(1871)*

____ (F) Why was it easy for people on the west coast to trade with the United States? Name two reasons. *(river valleys lay south and north; travel along the coast by ship was fast; mountains created a barrier - 2 out of 3)*

____ (F) Which country wanted the colony of British Columbia? *(United States)*

____ (F) Name three things that the American people have in common with British Columbians. *(mining; logging; ocean products; shipping – 3 out of 4)*

____ (F) Why did British Columbia join Canada rather than the United States? *(the Canadian government promised that a railway would be constructed)*

____ (F) Under what condition did British Columbia agree to enter into Confederation? *(the railway construction would commence in two years and be completed in ten)*

____ (I) Name two reasons why it was so expensive to build the railway. *(it was a ten year project; it required 9,000 employees; it required a lot of equipment; they blasted through rock; they built bridges - 2 out of 5 - **Say, "Please be more specific" if the student provides a general, vague answer**)*

____ (I) Why did the railway company bring 9000 men via ship from China? *(They were unable to recruit enough local men)*

____ (I) Name two ways in which the Chinese workers were disappointed. *(they were paid less than the other workers; the workers were not welcome to stay; the government refused to allow the families to enter country; the government refused to let Chinese women stay – 2 out of 4)*

____ (I) Why was the building of the railroad an unfortunate chapter in Canadian history? *(the Chinese workers were treated very poorly by the Canadians; many people died – 1 out of 2)*

READING LEVEL

Independent 9½ - 10 points	Instructional 7 - 9 points	Frustration 6½ points or less

PRIOR KNOWLEDGE
How much did you know about the construction of the Canadian railway before reading this passage?

I knew:

LEVEL OF INTEREST
How much did you like reading this passage?

Introduction: This is the story of a murder investigation.

Tracking a Killer

The dumpster was blackened but already cool to the touch. A dark stain extended from the bottom corner down onto the pavement of the parking lot. When the police first removed the metal cover of the dumpster, they saw nothing in the charred interior but a layer of ash covering the bottom. Looking again, they distinguished a body so badly burned they could not tell whether it was animal or human. They transferred the fragile remains of the body to a body bag and sent them to a pathology lab. The pathologist established that the victim was human – a white female in her early twenties. X-rays revealed a gunshot to the head.

Three days after the discovery of the body, the police received a call from a local bank teller. The teller told them that a nervous young woman had come into the bank to close her account, but then left suspiciously before the transaction was completed. The teller had asked her to wait while she confirmed the withdrawal, but the woman was already gone when the teller returned. The woman – and a man who had been waiting for her just outside the bank doors – were recorded clearly by the bank's video security system. The police made a copy of the video and broadcast it on the local news station. Someone came forward and identified the woman. When questioned, the woman said the man who had accompanied her to the bank offered her $500. To earn this money, she needed to pose as a friend of his and withdraw all the money from this friend's account. The woman knew nothing about a murder.

The male friend was questioned and his vehicle inspected thoroughly. The police discovered bloodstains on the rear and right side of the car, and a bloody tire iron and a .22 calibre gun hidden in the trunk. The police knew they had their murderer, but they had to make a concrete connection between him and the victim. They went back to the pathologist. The pathologist prepared two DNA profiles – one with cells from a molar extracted from the victim's jaw and another using cells obtained from the bloodstains found on the suspect's car. The profiles matched.

Confronted by the evidence, the suspect confessed. He said the victim had owed him money but refused to pay. One night the suspect offered the victim a ride home from a bar. He beat her, put her body in the trunk of his car, drove to the deserted industrial park, threw the victim in the dumpster, shot her in the head, and set her on fire using gasoline. He was convicted of second-degree murder and sentenced to life imprisonment.

(451 words)

RETELLING
Please retell the story.

COMPREHENSION

____ (I) What did the police see coming out of the bottom corner of the dumpster onto the pavement? *(blood)*

____ (F) Where was the dumpster located? *(in a deserted industrial park; in a parking lot – 1 out of 2)*

____ (F) What did the police see when they first removed the metal cover of the dumpster? *(ashes)*

____ (F) The police sent the body to a pathology lab. Name three pieces of information that the pathologist established about the victim. *(the victim was human; a white female; in her early twenties; killed by a gunshot to the head – 3 out of 4)*

____ (I) Who did the police receive the first clue from? *(the bank teller)*

____ (I) Why was the woman nervous about closing the account? *(it wasn't her account)*

____ (I) What was the victim doing before she was killed? *(listening to music in a bar; drinking in a bar - 1 out of 2)*

____ (F) Name three pieces of evidence that the police discovered in the car. *(bloodstains, a tire iron, and a gun)*

____ (I) What did the man beat the woman with? *(a tire iron)*

____ (I) What do you think this murderer could have done to reduce his chances of getting caught. Name two things. *(cleaned his car; hidden the gun; cleaned the tire iron; not gone to the bank - 2 out of 4)*

READING LEVEL

Independent 9½ - 10 points	Instructional 7 - 9 points	Frustration 6½ points or less

LEVEL OF INTEREST
How much did you like reading this story?

1	2	3	4
it was not interesting	it was fairly good	it was good	it was excellent

Introduction: This is a story about a woman's fortieth birthday adventure.

Not Bad for Forty!

Carla's birthday marked her 40th year of life. But had she really lived, she thought? She had heard others talk enthusiastically of holidays in Mexico. Impulsively, she booked an all-inclusive package to Mazatlan. She'd skip Christmas and all the hassle that went along with it. Her friend Marni agreed to accompany her.

The departure date saw two very excited women board the charter jet in -22 degree temperatures. The four-hour plane trip went quickly enough as Carla enjoyed the meal and a movie from her window seat. The Mexican resort was everything she had hoped it would be. The hotel was terrific, the food fantastic, and the weather hot! A constant wind blew from the Pacific Ocean, cooling the sunbathers by hotel pools and on sandy beaches. Vendors approached the basking tourists with every description of merchandise.

Carla and Marni had their hair braided and beaded by petite senoritas. They strolled the narrow sidewalks, stopping at shops and booths along the way. Little white golf-cart style cabs were cheap, enjoyable transportation, taking the adventurous duo to the world's highest lighthouse, the fishing docks, the cruise ship ports, and the famed fiestas of Mexican night life.

The week sped by. Carla held an iguana to pose for a picture on the beach, tried lobster for the first time ever, and topped it off with an exhilarating airborne escapade – parasailing. She was amazed at how fearlessly she slipped into the harness gear, receiving brief instruction in broken English. "Sit down like you sit on a toilet. Then run, but stay sitting…"

Easily said, a little awkward to accomplish! However the sky was hers as a motorboat gently towed the parachute into the wind and up over the ocean! The shoreline's many hotels were distinct in their shapes and colors. Thatched palm roofs of shade huts along the beach looked like little mushrooms sprouting from a sandy bed. Other brilliantly colored parasails dotted the sky in the distance. Ten minutes later, Carla spotted the instructor's flag, waving her in for the landing. She tugged the rope sling above her right arm, and the chute eased her down to earth again. "Ha!" she congratulated herself, "How's that for 40?"

Carla was extremely happy! She felt confident, content, and a little bit crazy as she sipped margaritas and counted her blessings.

(389 words)

RETELLING
Please retell the story.

COMPREHENSION

____ (I) What did Carla think was missing from her life? *(adventure; excitement – 1 out of 2)*

____ (I) What country did Carla depart from? *(accept Canada or the United States)*

____ (I) Do you think Carla was married? Explain your answer. *(no, she brought a girlfriend with her; no, if she was married her husband would have gone with her – 1 out of 2)*

____ (F) Name three things that Carla liked about the resort. *(terrific hotel, fantastic food, and hot weather)*

____ (F) Which ocean was the resort beside? *(the Pacific Ocean)*

____ (I) Describe the length of Carla's hair. *(accept shoulder-length or long)*

____ (F) What did they use for transportation in Mazatlan? *(little white golf-cart style cabs)*

____ (I) Name three incidents that showed the spontaneous and adventurous side of Carla's character. *(booking a package to Mazatlan; going parasailing; eating lobster for the first time; holding an iguana for the first time; getting hair braided and beaded – 3 out of 5)*

____ (F) How did Carla feel after the parasailing ride? Name two feelings. *(happy; confident; content; a little bit crazy – 2 out of 4)*

____ (I) At the end of the story, Carla counted her blessings. Name two of them. *(she had her health; she had extra money to go on a trip; she had a friend; she lived to 40; she had an adventure – 2 out of 5)*

READING LEVEL

Independent 9½ - 10 points	Instructional 7 - 9 points	Frustration 6½ points or less

LEVEL OF INTEREST
How much did you like reading this story?

1 —————— 2 —————— 3 —————— 4

it was not interesting	it was fairly good	it was good	it was excellent

Introduction: This is about baldness.

Baldness

The medical term used to describe permanent baldness is alopecia. The more common term is pattern baldness. Pattern baldness or permanent hair loss strikes men more than women. In fact, two out of three men develop some type of balding during their lifetime. For males, this condition tends to result in a receding hairline and baldness on the crown of the head. For females, pattern baldness is the thinning of hair over the entire scalp. Permanent hair loss is largely hereditary among both men and women. So if a person's ancestors were bald, chances are he or she will inherit the trait.

Hair loss can be temporary or permanent. Factors linked with short-term hair loss include stress, hormonal imbalance, an underactive or overactive thyroid, and chemotherapy. Diets that are low in protein or iron are also a factor. As well, women may experience short-term hair loss from menopause, the stress of childbirth, or as a side effect of using birth control pills.

In our society, a great deal of emphasis is placed on one's appearance. Consequently, watching a hairline recede can be traumatic. Pattern baldness has been known to affect one's self-esteem, motivation, self-image, and ultimately happiness. Many people who experience hair loss spend lots of time and attention, not to mention huge sums of money, to find a treatment or a cure.

There are several treatments for pattern baldness. An American organization called the Food and Drug Administration (FDA) approved a drug marketed as

Rogaine, which is available over the counter. Rogaine is a lotion that is rubbed into the scalp twice a day. Its effectiveness varies, and research shows that 25 to 30 percent of men experience some hair regrowth. The product seems to be most effective in early stages of hereditary baldness.

In 1998, the FDA approved Propecia, the first pill to treat male pattern hair loss effectively. In studies of 1,553 men, 86 percent of those taking the drug grew new hair or maintained their hair. This pill can be used only by men, as it poses a threat of birth defects among pregnant women. Like all prescription drugs, Propecia may cause side effects such as less desire for sex, difficulty in achieving an erection, and a decrease in the amount of semen.

Surgery is another alternative. Hair transplants are usually performed by dermatologists. They take tiny plugs of skin, each containing several hairs, from the back or side of the head. The plugs are then implanted into bald sections of scalp. Three or four transplants may be needed, at four-month intervals. Risk of infection is relatively high in this form of hair replacement. Another drawback of surgery is that this type of treatment is expensive and can also be very painful.

(462 words)

RETELLING
Please retell the passage.

COMPREHENSION

____ (I) In a group of six men, how many will develop some type of balding during their lifetime? *(four)*

____ (F) Name three factors that are linked with short-term hair loss. *(stress; hormonal imbalance; underactive thyroid; overactive thyroid; chemotherapy; diets low in protein; diets low in iron; menopause; the stress of childbirth; birth control pills - 3 out of 10)*

____ (I) Why might a strict vegetarian be prone to hair loss? *(the diet is low in protein)*

____ (F) What is the name of the organization in the United States that approves drugs? *(Food and Drug Administration)*

____ (I) Why do people who experience hair loss spend lots of time and money on finding a treatment or cure? Provide three reasons. *(baldness affects self-esteem; baldness affects motivation; baldness affects self-image; baldness affects happiness; improves appearance – 3 out of 5)*

____ (I) According to the author, when does Rogaine seem to be the most effective? *(in the early stages of hereditary baldness)*

____ (F) Name three side effects of Propecia. *(less desire for sex; difficulty in achieving an erection; a decrease in the amount of semen; birth defects – 3 out of 4)*

____ (I) Why is Rogaine safer than Propecia? *(Rogaine doesn't have any side effects; Rogaine is applied externally - 1 out of 2)*

____ (F) What are three disadvantages of hair transplants? *(infection; expensive; and painful; takes time - 3 out of 4)*

____ (F) Who usually performs hair transplants? *(dermatologists)*

READING LEVEL

Independent	Instructional	Frustration
$9\frac{1}{2}$ - 10 points	7 - 9 points	$6\frac{1}{2}$ points or less

PRIOR KNOWLEDGE
How much did you know about baldness before reading this passage?

I knew:

1 — nothing 2 — very little 3 — something 4 — a lot

LEVEL OF INTEREST
How much did you like reading this passage?

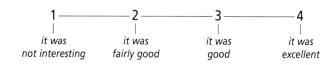

1 — it was not interesting 2 — it was fairly good 3 — it was good 4 — it was excellent

Introduction: This passage describes why birds can fly.

Why Can Birds Fly?

Only three groups of animals – birds, insects and bats – have acquired the power of true flight; that is, flight in which the wings are flapped rhythmically up and down to produce lift and thrust.

All fliers have to overcome similar problems. Air is such a thin medium, compared with water or earth, that travellers passing through it must have light bodies and wings to be able to maintain lift. They must also have a high "power/weight ratio." That is, their flight muscles must be extremely powerful in relation to their body weight. A pigeon's heart muscles, which operate its wings, account for more than a third of its body weight.

Birds have remarkably light skeletons. This lightness has been achieved without sacrificing strength. The skull bones of modern birds are very thin, and heavy teeth have been replaced by light, horny beaks. Long bones, such as those in the wings, are hollow, supported by a criss-crossing system of internal struts. The tail, which helps with steering, is formed entirely of that skin covering unique to birds – feathers.

Extremely light, flexible, and airproof, feathers are a miracle of flight technology. A "primary" or flight feather consists of a shaft or quill, hollow at its base for conveying nourishment, solid towards its tip for strength; and a vane made up of side shafts called barbs. These barbs, in turn, support rows of barbules, equipped with interlocking hooks to form a fine mesh surface for the feather. If the barbules break apart, the bird can reset them by preening, an important task which occupies much of a bird's time. Near the base of the tail, a bird has oil glands, the oil being used during preening and cleaning to coat the feathers, keeping them waterproof and buoyant. Together with the tail feathers, the primary feathers form an arched wing that provides lift and thrust, or reverse thrust when landing.

Birds require a complex nervous system to remain stable in flight. For this reason birds have relatively larger brains than all mammals (except primates), and the part of the brain that coordinates movement in particularly well developed.

Flying uses a lot of energy. Consequently, birds spend much of their time searching for food. Oxygen is also needed in large amounts, and birds have quite uniquely designed lungs with special air sacs, which surround the vital organs of the body and even penetrate certain wing bones. Inside these sacs, the air flows around a one-way system, enabling the bird to extract all the oxygen from one breath of air while at the same time expelling all carbon dioxide. The air sacs also allow the bird to lose the excessive heat produced during flight, and as a bonus, they reduce the density or solidity of its body.

(461 words)

RETELLING

Please retell the passage.

COMPREHENSION

_____ (F) What three groups of animals have acquired the power of true flight? *(birds, insects and bats)*

_____ (I) Name two reasons why birds can fly. *(they have a high power/weight ratio; light skeletons; light feathers; light bodies; light wings; powerful flight muscles – 2 out of 6)*

_____ (F) What does the term "high power/weight ratio" mean? *(the flight muscles are extremely powerful in relation to their body weight)*

_____ (I) Do you think a flying squirrel has acquired the power of true flight? Explain your answer. *(no, because it doesn't have wings)*

_____ (F) How do flight feathers convey nourishment? *(through the feather's hollow base)*

_____ (F) Which feathers provide lift and thrust? *(the primary and tail feathers)*

_____ (F) Describe the bones in the wing. Provide two descriptions. *(hollow; light; long; supported by a criss-crossing system of internal struts – 2 out of 4)*

_____ (F) Name two tasks that birds spend most of their time doing. *(preening and looking for food)*

_____ (I) Air sacs reduce the density or solidity of a bird's body. Why is this considered to be a bonus? *(it makes their bodies lighter)*

_____ (F) Name two benefits of air sacs. *(they allow the bird to lose heat; reduce density and solidity of its body; allow a one-way breathing system – 2 out of 3)*

READING LEVEL

Independent 9½ - 10 points	Instructional 7 - 9 points	Frustration 6½ points or less

PRIOR KNOWLEDGE

How much did you know about why birds can fly before reading this passage?

I knew:

1 — nothing   2 — very little   3 — something   4 — a lot

LEVEL OF INTEREST

How much did you like reading this passage?

1 — it was not interesting   2 — it was fairly good   3 — it was good   4 — it was excellent

Introduction: This is the story of the kidnapping of the child of a famous man.

The Suspect

They say the father searched the grounds of the estate desperately. He called the state police; and instantly droves of police, investigators, and reporters descended on the secluded mansion, possibly obliterating important evidence that might have been left behind. The investigators did find a rough, home-made ladder; a chisel; and a ransom note demanding $50,000, which they found on the window sill of the second-floor library – the last place where the parents claimed they had seen their 20-month-old son.

For a month, letters poured in – psychic predictions, death threats, and sympathy notes. The parents withdrew from sight in an attempt to avoid the constant curiosity of the public. A retired principal came forward saying that he had been in contact with the kidnapper and would act as an intermediary. He explained that because of a strong personal desire to see the kidnapped baby reunited with the parents, he had invested a thousand dollars of his own money in a newspaper ad that encouraged the kidnapper to contact him.

In April, one month after the abduction, the father and the retired principal met in a cemetery with the kidnapper. The principal handed the kidnapper $50,000 in marked bills and returned to the parked car where the father of the child waited anxiously. He produced a note that said the toddler was in a boat off the coast of Massachusetts. The information proved false. One month later, only a few miles away from the family mansion, a truck driver pulled over to the side of a country lane to relieve himself. He discovered the tiny body of the missing boy hidden under a pile of dead leaves – his skull fractured.

Two long years later, a traveller stopped at a gas station, purchased his gas with a single bill, and drove away. The proprietor of the gas station, suspecting that the bill might be counterfeit, jotted down the traveler's license plate number on the back of it and promptly reported the incident to the police. The bill turned out to be one of the marked bills from the cemetery transaction two years earlier. The license plate number led the police to the residence of a German-born carpenter with a criminal record, residing illegally in the United States. Further investigation led to the discovery of $14,000 hidden in the garage and a missing plank of wood from the attic floor. Was this man the kidnapper? The media and the public, after clamoring for justice for over two years, were ready to believe so. When the retired principal testified in court that the suspect was the man to whom he had given the $50,000 in the cemetery, the suspect's fate was sealed.

In spite of numerous doubts concerning the purely circumstantial evidence provided at the trial, Bruno Hauptman died in the electric chair in the spring of 1936, charged with kidnapping Charles Lindbergh Jr. – the child of the famous and beloved aviator, Charles Lindbergh.

(498 words)

RETELLING
Please retell the story.

COMPREHENSION

____ (F) Name three things the kidnapper left at the mansion? *(a ladder, a chisel, and a ransom note)*

____ (I) How do you know that the family was wealthy? *(they lived in a mansion; they lived in an estate; they gave the kidnapper $50,000; he was a famous aviator – 2 out of 4)*

____ (F) Name two kinds of letters that arrived after the kidnapping. *(psychic predictions; death threats; sympathy notes - 2 out of 3)*

____ (F) In his note, where did the kidnapper say the toddler was located? *(in a boat off the coast of Massachusetts)*

____ (I) When do you think the baby was murdered? *(shortly after he was kidnapped; in March; in 1934 – 1 out of 3)*

____ (I) Name two individuals who were involved in solving this case. *(the truck driver; the proprietor of the gas station; the principal - 2 out of 3)*

____ (I) Of the 50,000, how much money do you think Bruno spent? *($36,000)*

____ (I) What type of evidence did the police need to convict Bruno Hauptman? *(a murder weapon; a confession; an eyewitness; marked bills - 1 out of 4)*

____ (F) Explain the role of the principal. *(he acted as an intermediary; he gave the money to the kidnapper; he sealed the fate of the kidnapper - 2 out of 3 -* **Ask "What else?" if the student only provides one response)**

____ (I) Which individual from the story was responsible for convicting the German-born carpenter? *(the retired principal)*

READING LEVEL

Independent 9½ - 10 points	Instructional 7 - 9 points	Frustration 6½ points or less

LEVEL OF INTEREST
How much did you like reading this story?

1 —————— 2 —————— 3 —————— 4
| | | |
it was not interesting   *it was fairly good*   *it was good*   *it was excellent*

Introduction: This is a story about a mysterious loss.

Remembering Emily

An elderly man trudged along the dusty incline of a path that led to the knoll overlooking Newdale. For most of his life he had lived in the rolling landscape, near the southern boundaries of this rural village.

Now he looked down on his hometown to see the busy profile of a country fair, beckoning him toward its sounds and smells. Lucas Wicks gripped his walking cane with renewed strength and made his way down the slope. With each step, a memory crept into his aging mind.

Little Emily had been at the fair that day, 25 years ago. Lucas and his wife Margaret were busy at the jewellery store until late that afternoon. Emily pleaded, with her four-year-old insistence, until her parents conceded. "Very well, Emily. You must behave, and listen to what your Uncle Morris says," Lucas recalled his wife having chided. Morris was Margaret's younger brother and not of a responsible nature.

Emily's blonde ringlets bounced as she eagerly counted out her piggy bank money to buy cotton candy and ride tickets. The silver carnival charm bracelet, designed by her adoring father, jangled on her chubby wrist.

"Good-bye, Daddy." She kissed his cheek for the last time.

"You all right, Luke?" a voice interrupted the jeweller's thoughts. Lucas hadn't realized he'd reached the fairground gates and was standing mesmerized by the spinning ferris wheel. He positioned his portly frame on a nearby bench and answered his neighbor. "Sure Arty, just a little overheated." He wiped the sweat off his forehead with a swipe of his arm.

Resting in the shade, Lucas again drifted into the past. His precious Emily had been kidnapped that day, at this very fairground. Years of investigation had never developed a successful lead as to her whereabouts, and Lucas had never forgiven his brother-in-law for his incompetence in caring for his rambunctious niece that fateful day. Margaret had taken her own life only months later. Lucas had dejectedly continued at his jewellery store until his retirement five years ago. From his watchband sparkled a tangible memory of his treasured daughter–a tiny carousel charm that was the identical mate to one he had crafted for his child. Suddenly a gentle tap on his shoulder pulled Lucas from his reverie. He raised tired eyes to see a vision. Before him stood the replica of his unforgettable Emily. Golden curls cascaded around rosy cheeks. The cherub pointed to the awestruck senior's wristwatch.

"I have a merry-go-round just like you," she chortled, holding out her arm to display the unique charm bracelet Lucas had designed many years before. Behind the child stood her mother, so unmistakable was the likeness. Hardly daring to hope, Lucas rose slowly from the bench. "Emily, is it you?" he whispered. He thought he saw a momentary glimmer of recognition in her eyes. "No, my name is Mary," she answered as she gathered up her child and turned to go.

(495 words)

RETELLING
Please retell the story.

COMPREHENSION

___ (I) Why do you think the kidnappers took Emily? *(the kidnappers wanted a daughter)*

___ (F) Name two things that Emily wanted to buy at the fair. *(cotton candy and ride tickets)*

___ (I) One of the charms on Emily's silver carnival charm bracelet was a merry-go round. What other charm do you think would have been on the bracelet? *(accept any answer related to a carnival, e.g., a clown, a Ferris wheel)*

___ (I) Who was responsible for the disappearance of Emily? *(Uncle Morris; Margaret's brother; Lucas's brother-in-law - 1 out of 3)*

___ (F) How does the author describe Uncle Morris? *(irresponsible)*

___ (I) Why did Arty ask Luke if he was all right? *(because Luke was mesmerized; because Luke was sweating - 1 out of 2)*

___ (F) Describe the physical appearance of Lucas. *(elderly; used a cane; portly - 2 out of 3)*

___ (F) Describe Emily's appearance. *(blonde ringlets; chubby; rosy cheeks; cherub - 2 out of 4 -* **Ask "What else?" if the student provides only one description)**

___ (I) Why did Luke think Mary was his daughter? Provide two reasons. *(the child's and Luke's carousel were identical; Mary's child resembled Emily; glimmer of recognition in her eyes – 1 out of 3)*

___ (I) If Emily were alive, how old would she be? *(29)*

READING LEVEL

Independent 9½ - 10 points	Instructional 7 - 9 points	Frustration 6½ points or less

LEVEL OF INTEREST
How much did you like reading this story?

1 — it was not interesting 2 — it was fairly good 3 — it was good 4 — it was excellent

Introduction: This is about beans.

Beans

The benefits of beans have been recognized since people first began to cultivate their food. In the Middle East beans were cultivated about 8000 B.C., and in China soybeans were cultivated earlier than 3000 B.C. Beans were very popular in ancient Greece and Rome. In fact, they were used for counting votes in ancient Rome. Beans have been eaten around the world for over 10,000 years and are still a staple in many countries.

Bean dishes are eaten daily by the majority of the people throughout the Middle East, North Africa, and South and Central America. In East Asia soybeans are used extensively, mostly in the forms of bean curd, miso, and tamari. Bean curd, which is produced from soybean milk, and tamari, a naturally fermented soy sauce, are used throughout East Asia. Miso, a fermented soybean paste, is used as a soup base and a seasoning mainly in Japan.

Beans, an important source of nutrients, contain iron, B vitamins, folic acid, calcium, magnesium, and potassium and are the best plant source of protein. This food source is high in dietary fibre, low in saturated fat, and cholesterol-free. Dried beans are also a healthy food choice because they are not subjected to the preservatives or other chemicals generally used in processed foods.

Beans are so pretty and decorative that people are tempted to line them up in glass jars on a countertop. This temptation should be resisted, however, as beans stay fresher longer when they are stored in a dark place. Ideally, beans should be stored in glass bottles or plastic bags in a cupboard or drawer located as far as possible from the oven – in the coolest, driest place in the kitchen. The beans should be consumed within six months, as older beans absorb more water during the cooking process and take longer to become tender.

Although beans are very nutritious, many people tend to avoid them because they produce gas. The bean contains sugars, which are at the root of the intestinal problems attributed to beans. The stomach does not contain the enzymes needed to digest these sugars in the small intestine, so the sugars arrive in the large intestine undigested. The bacteria that live in the large intestine feed off and ferment these sugars, producing carbon dioxide, hydrogen, and a few other gases as by-products.

There are a few ways to reduce 60 percent of the gas produced from the sugars in beans. Soaking the beans in water permits the gas-producing sugars to be released. Gas is also reduced by discarding the water that the beans are soaked in, and by changing the water that beans are cooked in after 40 minutes. As well, a product marketed as Beano, which is available in most supermarkets and pharmacies, reduces gas production, as it contains an enzyme that assists in the digestion of sugars.

(481 words)

RETELLING
Please retell the passage.

COMPREHENSION

____ (I) Where did the expression "bean counters" come from? *(beans were used in Rome to count votes)*

____ (F) Name three places where beans are eaten daily by the majority of the people. *(Middle East; North Africa; South America; Central America – 3 out of 4)*

____ (I) Which bean is processed into several different food products? *(soybean)*

____ (F) In East Asia, soybeans are processed into different food products. Name three of them. *(bean curd, miso, and tamari)*

____ (F) How is miso used? *(as a soup base; a seasoning – 1 out of 2)*

____ (F) Name three nutrients that beans contain. *(protein; iron; B vitamins; calcium; magnesium; potassium – 3 out of 6)*

____ (F) Name three reasons why beans are a healthy food choice. *(high in nutrients; high in dietary fibre; low in saturated fat; cholesterol-free; not subjected to preservatives; not subjected to chemicals – 3 out of 6)*

____ (I) What are two adjustments that need to be made in preparing older beans? *(require longer cooking time and more water)*

____ (F) Name two types of gases that are produced in the large intestine. *(carbon dioxide and hydrogen)*

____ (F) Name three ways to reduce the gas produced from the sugars in beans. *(soak them in water; discard the water the beans are soaked in; change the water that beans are cooked in after 40 minutes; use Beano – 3 out of 4)*

READING LEVEL

Independent $9\frac{1}{2}$ - 10 points	Instructional 7 - 9 points	Frustration $6\frac{1}{2}$ points or less

PRIOR KNOWLEDGE
How much did you know about beans before reading this passage?

I knew:

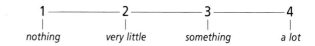

1 ——————— 2 ——————— 3 ——————— 4
nothing   very little   something   a lot

LEVEL OF INTEREST
How much did you like reading this passage?

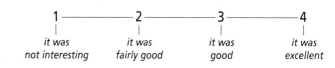

1 ——————— 2 ——————— 3 ——————— 4
it was   it was   it was   it was
not interesting   fairly good   good   excellent

Introduction: This is about women and osteoporosis.

Women and Osteoporosis

Osteoporosis, a condition of decreased bone mass, is one of the most common diseases affecting women. It leads to fragile bones that are at an increased risk of fracture. As the disease progresses, the spinal column can decrease in length, causing a height loss of several inches. The spine can also become curved as a result of fractures caused by the pressure of body weight on the deteriorating vertebrae.

The term "porosis" means spongy, which describes the appearance of osteoporosis bones when they are broken in half to examine them. Normal bone marrow has small holes within it, but a bone with osteoporosis will have much larger holes. Decreased bone mass is mainly caused by a decrease in the calcium content of the bones.

Those with the highest risk factor for osteoporosis are usually slender, small-boned Caucasian or Asian women who have exercised very little and taken in insufficient calcium during their growing years. The profile of women at risk also includes those who smoke and drink alcohol excessively. Finally, the chances of osteoporosis seem to increase dramatically with age, since a woman's bone mass normally peaks at age 35, after which she tends to lose about 1 percent of bone mass per year.

Osteoporosis is different from most other diseases or common illnesses in that there is no one single cause. The overall health of a person's bones is a function of many factors, ranging from how well the bones were formed in youth to the level of exercise the bones have seen over the years. One prevailing theory maintains that the disease results from a loss of the female hormone estrogen. This loss affects the calcium content of bones. Therefore, menopause and the removal of ovaries or uterus may lead to osteoporosis.

Osteoporosis can usually be prevented with some simple lifestyle changes. Regular and frequent weight-bearing exercise is one of the best strategies for increasing bone mass. Running, walking, and weight-lifting stimulate bone-cell production. Most doctors recommend about thirty minutes of exercise about three to five times per week.

As this disease often originates in a calcium deficiency, women should pay special attention to their calcium intake. The daily recommended dietary calcium intake varies by age, sex, and menopausal status. If women have difficulty consuming dairy products, there are other calcium-rich foods that should be included in their diet. Beans, especially kidney and pinto, and tofu are rich in calcium and protein. Good sources of calcium also include broccoli, nuts, figs, prunes, salmon, sardines, and leafy greens. Vitamins C and D increase the body's absorption of calcium. Coffee and tea should be avoided, as they promote the excretion of calcium through the urine.

For women at menopause, the appropriate administration of estrogen is the most potent means by which bone mass may be preserved. In fact, correction of low reproductive hormone levels at any age is important if proper bone mass is to be maintained. There is no one treatment or combination of treatments that can guarantee zero risk of fractures due to osteoporosis. The best prevention, however, is a life-long commitment to physical activity, good nutrition, and normal reproductive hormone status. (531 words)

RETELLING
Please retell the passage.

COMPREHENSION

____ (I) How would you know if a woman had a severe case of osteoporosis? *(she would shrink in height by several inches; she would be hunched over; bones would easily break - 1 out of 3)*

____ (F) What is the main cause of decreased bone mass? *(a decrease in the calcium content of bones)*

____ (F) Name three things that can lead to osteoporosis. *(poor bone formation during youth; lack of exercise; low estrogen level; calcium deficiency; excessive smoking; excessive drinking - 3 out of 6)*

____ (I) Why would a woman at the age of 50 be at an increased risk for osteoporosis? *(she would be going through menopause, which decreases the estrogen levels in the body)*

____ (F) At what age does a woman's bone mass peak? *(35)*

____ (F) Name three types of exercise that stimulate bone cell production. *(weight-lifting, running, and walking)*

____ (F) The recommended daily calcium intake varies by three factors. What are they? *(age, sex and menopausal status)*

____ (F) If you have difficulty consuming dairy products, what are five things you can eat to increase your calcium intake? *(beans; tofu; broccoli; nuts; figs; prunes; salmon; sardines; leafy greens - 5 out of 9)*

____ (I) Do you think that osteoporosis is a common disease among men? Explain. *(no, men don't have the hormone estrogen which plays a role in osteoporosis)*

____ (F) For women at menopause, what is the most potent means to preserve bone mass? *(the appropriate administration of estrogen)*

READING LEVEL

Independent	Instructional	Frustration
$9\frac{1}{2}$ - 10 points	7 - 9 points	$6\frac{1}{2}$ points or less

PRIOR KNOWLEDGE
How much did you know about osteoporosis before reading this passage?

I knew:

LEVEL OF INTEREST
How much did you like reading this passage?

The Big One

The men spilled silently from the 1949 green Ford truck parked at the far end of the playground, which adjoined the building, and waited. Nobody spoke, but they were deeply aware of each other's constant upward glances, the slow, steadying intakes of breath, the subtle shifting of weight from one foot to the other and back again. When a quick flash of light from the roof of a tenement building overlooking the targeted building pierced the evening sky, the seven armed men moved in unified silence through the playground and down the quiet street until they huddled momentarily in the darkened entrance of the building. Using the copy of the outside door key that they had previously obtained from an unsuspecting locksmith, the gloved men entered quickly, donning their Halloween masks and chauffeur caps. Wordlessly, they made their way directly to the vault room on the second floor, where they knew five employees were engaged in their nightly chore of checking and storing the payrolls and deliveries that had been entrusted to their care that day. They unlocked the vault room door with one of the many other keys in their possession and easily overpowered the unsuspecting employees, expertly binding and gagging them with rope and adhesive tape.

The robbers moved through the room performing their assigned tasks silently, like dancers stepping effortlessly through a familiar choreography. The practiced routine was interrupted only once, but completely unexpectedly, by the sound of a warning buzzer. One of the robbers quickly removed the adhesive tape from the mouth of one employee and learned that the buzzer indicated that someone wanted access to the vault area. Two of the other gang members immediately positioned themselves near the sole door in the room, guns poised, ready to nab the intruder. For some reason, the would-be victim strolled past the vault, seemingly unconcerned, so they let him be. The two gang members returned to their work, but instinctively they all moved more swiftly pushed by a stronger sense of urgency.

The gang loaded their hefty bags of loot into the waiting getaway vehicle, which was now parked according to schedule at the front entrance of the building. They clambered into the back of it, and as they made their escape, the five employees in the vault room worked themselves free and reported the crime. They didn't know it at the time, but they had just witnessed the crime of the century.

The robbers had succeeded in stealing $1.2 million in cash and $1.5 million in checks, money orders, and other securities from the "impenetrable" Brinks building at 165 Prince Street in Boston, Massachusetts. Total time of the heist? Less than five minutes.

(450 words)

RETELLING
Please retell the story.

COMPREHENSION

____ (F) What was the year, colour, and make of the vehicle they used? *(1949 green Ford)*

____ (I) Why did the robbers use a truck for a getaway vehicle? *(they needed a large vehicle for the gang and the loot)*

____ (I) How did the robbers know when it was safe to enter the Brinks building? *(there was a quick flash of light from the roof of a tenement building; one of the men was watching from the roof of a tenement building – 1 out of 2)*

____ (F) Who made the copy of the outside door key? *(a locksmith)*

____ (I) How many keys do you think the locksmith made? *(accept any answer that indicates more than two)*

____ (F) Name three things that the robbers were wearing. *(gloves, Halloween masks, and chauffeur caps)*

____ (I) Why were the robbers able to easily overpower the employees? *(there were more robbers than employees; there were seven robbers and five employees; the employees were unsuspecting; the robbers were armed – 1 out of 4)*

____ (F) What did the warning buzzer indicate? *(someone wanted access to the vault area)*

____ (I) Seven of the nine robbers entered the building. What were the responsibilities of the other two robbers? *(one gave the signal to enter the building and one drove the getaway vehicle)*

____ (I) Name two things that you think were remarkable about this robbery. *(they succeeded in stealing money from a building that was supposed to be impossible to rob; the robbery took less than five minutes; nobody was hurt; the large amount of money they stole – 2 out of 4)*

READING LEVEL

Independent 9½ - 10 points	Instructional 7 - 9 points	Frustration 6½ points or less

LEVEL OF INTEREST
How much did you like reading this story?

1 ——————— 2 ——————— 3 ——————— 4

it was not interesting	*it was fairly good*	*it was good*	*it was excellent*

Introduction: This story is about a secret from long ago.

Secret of Significance

Standing elegantly against the papered wall of Helen's massive bedroom, a lustrous maple armoire gleamed in silent splendor. Helen was still basking in the pleasure of finding such a treasure abandoned in a dusty corner of the Ericksons' farmhouse attic. The retiring couple had gladly parted with the monstrosity that had been a gift to Daniel Erickson's mother, Edna. "Mom said the cabinetmaker was an old acquaintance and the wardrobe was the only thing she'd ever really owned." Daniel shook his head sadly, remembering how cruelly his father had treated his mother and himself. "Father despised the thing and insisted it be out of sight immediately after Mom passed away over thirty-five years ago."

Helen was appalled that a quality piece of craftsmanship should be hated and hidden by the elder Mr. Erickson, but elated that the immaculately polished antique was now in her possession. Carefully she measured and clipped rectangles of lavender scented drawer liners before placing her own personal items into their historical time capsule. Blouses, scarves, jewelry, journals, and stationery – each had a fragrant storage spot. Removing the bottom drawer, she noticed a yellowed sheet of parchment flutter to the floor. The edges were brittle, but the writing appeared barely faded as Helen reached for the letter addressed to Edna Abernathy. Blushing, she realized the object of her curiosity was indeed a love letter to the deceased Mrs. Erickson. She envisioned a young woman dressed in the fashion of 1931, as indicated by the date in the upper corner of the document. Helen nestled into a gigantic wooden rocker near the window, and journeyed into the past through the author's captivating letter...

My beloved Edna,

How my heart and being yearns for you as your wedding day approaches. My future is dismal and worthless without your tenderness, beauty, passion, and companionship. This dastardly villain to whom you are betrothed is sure to make our lives miserable and destitute. It wrenches my heart to know your father is merely satisfying his greed with this arrangement, and it is beyond my power to alter it.

I have lovingly constructed an armoire for you to remember me by, built with some significance. Seven drawers represent the months of love we shared, and each shall house the secret of our affair. The tightly grained maple wood shall remind you of our embraces as you caress its smoothness with your gentle fingers. Its pleasant aroma is reminiscent of the fragrant forest floor on which we reclined to contemplate the starlit skies and our unfulfilled future. The rod supporting your garments has been hewn from the strongest of branches, one that reached to the heavens; through this column, your sweetness shall be transported to me. Each hinge and handle is of brass – an alloy of strength, pliability, and beauty; this is our love for each other even in separate lives. Engraved above, below, and upon its door are complicated symbols of lions, for which you shall have a lifetime of memories. My request, before taking my own life, is that you name our son Daniel, for he shall have lions to battle.

I shall be waiting, my precious Edna,

Yours in life and in death,

Sullivan McMasters

(535 words)

RETELLING
Please retell the story.

COMPREHENSION

____ (F) Where did Helen find the armoire?
(in the Erickson's farmhouse attic)

____ (I) How many years had the armoire been in the farmhouse attic? *(35 years)*

____ (I) Do you think Daniel knew the identity of his real father? Explain your answer. *(no, he thought the cabinetmaker was an old acquaintance of his mother; no, he wouldn't have given away the armoire if he knew his father built it – 1 out of 2)*

____ (F) Name three items that Helen stored in the armoire. *(blouses; scarves; jewellery; journals; stationery - 3 out of 5)*

____ (I) When did Sullivan commit suicide? *(just before Edna's wedding; 1931; after he wrote the letter; after he gave Edna the armoire - 1 out of 4)*

____ (F) What did the tightly grained maple wood remind Sullivan of? *(their embraces)*

____ (F) Why did Sullivan use brass handles and hinges? *(the strength, pliability, and beauty of brass represented their love)*

____ (I) In his letter, what words did Sullivan use to describe Edna's character? *(tender; sweet; passionate – 2 out of 3)*

____ (I) Describe Sullivan's character. *(passionate; romantic; tragic; intense; sentimental; affectionate; caring; gentle; loving; thoughtful; poetic – 2 out of 11 – **Ask "What else?" if the student only provides one response**)*

____ (I) Why did Sullivan McMasters think that Daniel would have lions to battle? *(Edna's husband might realize that Daniel was not his child; Edna was marrying an abusive man; Daniel will lead a difficult life with his stepfather; Daniel's stepfather was cruel - 1 out of 4)*

READING LEVEL

Independent 9½ - 10 points	Instructional 7 - 9 points	Frustration 6½ points or less

LEVEL OF INTEREST
How much did you like reading this story?

1	2	3	4
it was not interesting	it was fairly good	it was good	it was excellent

Section Six

Development of Graded Word Lists

Flo and I randomly selected the items for ADRI's graded word lists from the word lists of eight informal reading inventories (Bader, 1983; Burns & Roe, 1985; Ekwall, 1986; Johns, 1997; Leslie & Caldwell, 1990; Manzo, Manzo & McKenna, 1995; Silveroli, 1994; Steiglitz, 1992). Using these inventories, we developed a pool of 100 possible items for the graded word list. We used the *Word Frequency Book* (Carroll, Davies & Richman, 1971) to estimate word frequency for each of the 100 items and to group the items into nine word lists. The average frequency of the lists was determined using the Standard Frequency Index in the *Word Frequency Book* (see Table 1).

Table 1: Mean Standard Frequency Index for Word Lists									
Word List	**1**	**2**	**3**	**4**	**5**	**6**	**7**	**8**	**9**
MSF	65.21	62.12	55.12	51.15	49.68	44.36	40.89	37.58	22.25

We conducted a pilot study, using 46 adult basic education students, to determine the relationship between performance on the graded word list and the graded reading passages.

We posed this question: If the student correctly identified 90 percent of the words on a list, was he/she able to meet the criteria for instructional reading level at the same level? For example, if the student identified 90 percent of the words on the Level 5 list, was he/she able to meet the criteria for instructional reading level on a Level 5 passage?

The findings from the pilot study showed that if a student identified 90 percent of the words on a list, he/she obtained instructional reading level at the same level in 67 percent of the cases.

The correct entry level was overestimated by one level in 24 percent of the cases and underestimated by one level in 4 percent of the cases. Finally, the correct entry level was overestimated by two grade levels in 4 percent of the cases. These results indicate that the graded word list is an appropriate tool for predicting a student's entry level into the graded passages.

We also used the results of the pilot study to make minor changes in the items of the graded word list. Four words were replaced because the findings indicated that they were too difficult.

Development of the Graded Passages

We established student focus groups to determine the reading interests of adult basic education students. We hired adult educators in western, central, eastern and northern Canada to organize and facilitate 24 student focus groups. In Alberta, focus groups were located in Lethbridge, Vermilion, and Slave Lake. In Ontario, the settings were Dryden, Sudbury and Sioux Lookout. In Nova Scotia, the locations were Upper Hammonds Plains, Halifax, Dartmouth, Lawrencetown, and New Glasgow and in Newfoundland, the locations were Grand Falls-Windsor, and Clarenville. Finally, in the Northwest Territories, focus groups were situated in Cambridge Bay, Arctic Bay, Iqaluit, Fort Simpson, Inuvik, and Yellowknife. We used the data that emerged from these groups to determine the passage genre and topics for the informal reading inventory.

Each group was balanced in terms of the students' reading levels (beginning, intermediate and advanced). The composition of the student groups reflected the composition of ABE classes in western, central, eastern and northern Canada. In northern Canada, for example, the student groups were comprised of Inuit, Dene, Inuvialuit and Métis students (see Table 2).

Table 2: Composition of the Student Focus Groups					
	ALL	WEST	EAST	NORTH	CENTRAL
SAMPLE SIZE	200	48	70	46	36
Male	39%	44%	37%	28%	49%
Female	61%	56%	63%	72%	51%
Beginning Reader	27%	19%	26%	30%	38%
Intermediate Reader	42%	35%	44%	48%	35%
Advanced Reader	31%	46%	30%	20%	27%
Immigrant	19%	33%	14%	---	32%
Indigenous	30%	17%	---	100%	19%
Canadian born non-indigenous	51%	50%	86%	---	49%
Urban	53%	54%	56%	39%	65%
Rural	47%	46%	44%	61%	35%

The data that emerged from the focus groups suggested that the majority of students preferred reading informational passages more than narrative (6:1 ratio). Therefore, we decided that four informational and two narrative passages would be written for each of Levels 1 to 9. The students ranked mystery, adventure, romance, and true crime as their favorite narrative topics; and health, cooking, cultures, history, sports, animals, and personal development as their favorite informational topics.

We hired six individuals to write a total of 100 passages that reflected these topics. A set of criteria was developed for the writers that included the following semantic and syntactic factors: number of clauses, prepositional phrases and modifiers, referential cohesion, voice, vocabulary, and concept density. We also specified the length of each passage for Levels 1 to 9. After we evaluated the 100 passages for interest level, cohesion, and style, a total of 54 passages were selected for inclusion in ADRI. Two formulas – the Fry (Fry, 1977) and the Dale-Chall (Chall & Dale, 1995) – were applied to measure the readability levels of each passage.

We modified the Dale-Chall formula according to the following criteria: if a key concept from the title was repeated throughout the passage and was not included on the Dale-Chall list of familiar words, we did not count it as an unfamiliar word after its initial appearance. We modified the Fry formula in a similar manner: if a key concept from the title was repeated throughout the passage, we counted it as one syllable only after its initial appearance.

We wrote a set of inferential and factual comprehension questions for each passage. Dr. Grace Malicky, a reading specialist, analyzed whether each question was inferential or factual. The Arrington formula was used to determine the rate of agreement between Dr. Malicky and the developer of the questions. The rate of agreement was .9591. We modified some of the questions in order to increase the rate of agreement.

Pilot 1

We conducted a pilot study to determine the passage dependency of the comprehension questions. The sample consisted of 216 adult basic education students from colleges and community-based programs in Nova Scotia, Alberta, Ontario, and the Northwest Territories. A team of adult basic education instructors administered a set of two passages to each student. The instructors asked each student the comprehension questions prior to having him/her read the passage. We analyzed students' responses and revised correctly answered questions so that they would become passage dependent questions.

Pilot 2

We conducted the second pilot study to analyze the difficulty of the comprehension questions, to determine acceptable responses for each inference question and to determine whether any of the passages were too difficult or easy.

A team of adult basic education instructors administered ADRI to 962 students from community colleges and community-based programs situated in large communities (population greater than 65,000) and small communities (population less than 65,000) in northern, eastern, western, and central Canada. The students represented a cross-section of indigenous, Canadian-born, non-indigenous, and immigrant populations.

The instructors received training from us on how to administer ADRI. In order to ensure standardization, each ABE instructor followed a set of instructions and a script as he/she administered the test. We listened to an audio-tape of each instructor's first assessment to ensure that the instructions and script were followed. We kept in contact with the instructors every week to answer their questions, provide suggestions, and monitor their work.

Through a process of random sampling, we assigned a set of two narrative passages to 320 students, and a set of two informational passages to 642 students. If the student scored lower than 70 percent on the first passage he/she read, the instructor administered a set of lower passages. If the student scored higher than 90 percent, the instructor administered a set of higher level passages. Of the 962 students, 129 students scored at their frustration level on the first assigned passage they read and on the second assigned passage that was at a lower level. Consequently, we discarded their tests because the students did not perform at the instructional level. The remaining 833 students constituted the sample for this pilot study (see Table 3).

Table 3: Demographic Information for Sample of 833 Students									
	Female	Male	Canadian born*	Immigrant	Indigen-ous**	North	West	Central	East
Level 1	41	42	34	28	21	13	27	34	9
Level 2	42	39	38	15	28	13	22	44	2
Level 3	55	39	44	25	25	15	19	52	8
Level 4	57	39	46	30	20	12	27	49	8
Level 5	64	39	54	28	21	8	36	51	8
Level 6	59	43	57	28	20	13	29	50	10
Level 7	56	31	57	11	19	15	18	49	5
Level 8	48	42	66	8	16	12	31	43	4
Level 9	64	33	76	9	12	11	26	48	12

*This refers to non-indigenous individuals who were born in Canada
**This includes Dene, Inuit, Métis, and Inuvialuit students

The instructor who administered the test scored the comprehension questions for each passage that was read by the 833 students. Then, in order to ensure consistency, a graduate student rescored all of the instructors' tests. When the graduate student noticed discrepancies between her score and the instructors' scores, she discussed the discrepancy with us.

We worked with a statistician from the Center for Research in Applied Measurement and Evaluation (CRAME) at the University of Alberta to determine the degree of difficulty for the 586 comprehension questions from the 54 passages. We used a classical item analysis to obtain the proportion of individuals who scored either 0, 1/2 or 1 point on the comprehension questions. The findings indicated that many of the questions were either too difficult or too easy. Therefore, we modified these questions.

We also used the second pilot study to determine acceptable responses for each inference question. We analyzed students' responses for each inference question and then added appropriate responses to the answer key.

Finally, we used the second pilot study to determine whether any of the passages were too difficult or easy. We examined the students' comprehension scores and identified three passages that required rewriting.

Pilot 3

We used this study to determine whether a student's performance was consistent if he/she read a set of narrative passages or a set of informational passages at the same level. A secondary purpose of this study was to determine the degree of difficulty for the revised comprehension questions.

A total of 227 female and 132 male students from rural and urban Ontario whose mother tongue was English, participated in this pilot study. Five adult basic education instructors received training from Pat Campbell prior to administering the test. The instructor administered two narrative passages from an assigned level to 179 students and a set of four informational passages from an assigned level to 180 students.

When we compared the students' total comprehension scores across each level, we decided to delete one informational passage from each level because it was more difficult than the other three informational passages.

We then determined the degree of difficulty for the 400 comprehension questions in the remaining 45 passages. We used a classical item analysis to obtain the proportion of individuals who scored either 0, 1/2 or 1 point on the comprehension questions. Using this information, we replaced 6 questions, modified the wording of 17 questions and added responses for 32 inference questions and 8 factual questions. We found that it is difficult to predict responses for inference questions, because background knowledge affects how a person responds. This explains why we needed to add responses to 32 inference questions. We recalculated the students' comprehension scores for the 32 inference and 8 factual questions.

We then compared the students' mean comprehension score across the narrative and informational passages within each level. We generated mean scores, which are expressed in percentages, and standard deviations (See Tables 4 and 5). The results of this comparison suggests that the informational and narrative passages are parallel in terms of difficulty. For the American version, we deleted an additional informational passage containing Canadian content.

Table 4: Mean for Total Comprehension Score for Narrative Passages			
	MEAN	**S.D.**	**N**
Level 1 - HARD			
The End	.74	.11	19
Ted and the Cop	.76	.11	19
Level 2			
Bad Food	.77	.16	20
Rock and Roll	.82	.14	20
Level 3			
Summer Romance	.80	.12	20
The Piano Lesson	.79	.14	20
Level 4			
The Unlucky Bank Robber	.84	.12	20
Silent Watcher	.81	.08	20
Level 5			
Fire and a Friend	.73	.11	20
The Star Witness	.75	.09	20
Level 6			
Midnight Intruder	.81	.12	20
Greta's Vigil	.74	.11	20
Level 7			
Tracking a Killer	.73	.12	20
Not Bad for Forty	.77	.10	20
Level 8			
The Suspect	.75	.10	20
Remembering Emily	.79	.11	20
Level 9			
The Big One	.76	.11	20
Secret of Significance	.73	.12	20

Table 5: Mean for Total Comprehension Score for Informational Passages

	MEAN	S.D.	N
Level 1 - HARD			
Losing Body Fat	.76	.14	20
Ants	.77	.1	20
Level 2			
AIDS	.75	.13	20
The Polar Bear	.75	.12	20
Level 3			
The Queen Bee	.79	.14	20
A Pioneer Woman	.81	.11	20
Level 4			
Hay Fever	.76	.13	20
Beaver Lodges	.77	.13	20
Level 5			
Supermarket Temptations	.73	.10	20
Goalies	.74	.13	20
Level 6			
High Blood Pressure	.76	.06	20
Hanukkah	.79	.10	20
Level 7			
Food Poisoning	.76	.09	20
Finishing the Railroad	.77	.16	20
Level 8			
Baldness	.75	.07	20
Why Can Birds Fly?	.70	.09	20
Level 9			
Beans	.70	.11	20
Women and Osteoporosis	.74	.08	20

Development of Level 1 Easy Passages

Through discussions with the advisory committee and the instructors who administered the test, we decided that ADRI would be enhanced by developing a set of Level 1 easy passages. The Level 1 easy passages were administered to two basic education beginner students to determine whether a student's performance was consistent across the three narrative passages (See Table 6). The results of this comparison suggests that the narrative passages are parallel in terms of difficulty. The limitation of this pilot study was the small sample size.

– Pat Campbell

Table 6: Comparison of Comprehension Scores for Narrative Passages		
STUDENT	**STORY**	**COMPREHENSION**
A	Mary and her Son Joe Gets a Dog Sam and Pat	100% 80% 80%
B	Mary and her Son Joe Gets a Dog Sam and Pat	80% 80% 100%

Glossary

Cloze	Cloze is a procedure that omits portions of a text and asks readers to supply the missing elements. Typically, single words are omitted and replaced with blanks of a standard length. Sometimes, the cloze exercise omits word endings or single letters. The reader uses context clues and background knowledge to predict the missing elements.
Genre	Genre refers to different types of writing. ADRI uses two different genres: information and narrative.
Inference	A reader makes an inference whenever he/she "reads between the lines." An inference is a reasoned assumption about meaning that is not directly stated in the text.
Inference question	An inference question requires the reader to use his/her background knowledge and experience and the text information. In other words, the answer to an inference question cannot be located directly in the text.
Oral miscue	An oral miscue occurs when a person reads something different from what is printed in the text he/she is reading. A person's miscues are not random, and a pattern generally emerges. This pattern will provide information on how the person reads. This information, in turn, will assist the instructor in selecting appropriate instructional strategies.
Retelling	A retelling occurs when a student retells the passage he/she has just read in his/her own words.
Word blitzing	This strategy involves having a student brainstorm words about a particular topic. The student is then asked to group these words according to meaning and/or word structure.
Word family	Words that rhyme and contain the same word patterns belong to a word family. A word pattern is a common cluster of letters. For example, "ake" is a common word pattern, and its word family consists of make, take, lake, bake, etc.
Word sort	The purpose of word sort exercises is to have the student use word structure (familiar letter patterns, root words, syllables, prefixes and suffixes) to classify and compare words.

REFERENCES

Bader, L.A. (1983). <u>Bader reading and language inventory.</u>
New York: Macmillan.

Burns, P.C. & Roe, B.D. (1985). <u>Burns/Roe informal reading inventory.</u>
Boston: Houghton Mifflin Company.

Campbell, P. & Brokop, F. (1998). <u>Supplemental training for practitioners in literacy education.</u> Edmonton: Grass Roots Press.

Carroll, J.B., Davies, P. & Richman, B. (1971). <u>Word frequency book.</u>
Boston: Houghton Mifflin Company.

Chall, J.S. & Dale, E. (1995). <u>Manual for the new Dale-Chall readability formula.</u>
Massachusetts: Brookline Books.

Ekwall, E.E. (1986). <u>Ekwall reading inventory.</u>
Toronto: Allyn and Bacon, Inc.

Fry, E. (1977). <u>Fry's readability graph: Clarifications, validity and extension to level 17.</u> Journal of Reading, 21, 242-252.

Johns, J.L. (1997). <u>Basic reading inventory.</u>
Iowa: Kendall/hunt Publishing Company.

Leslie, L. & Caldwell, J. (1990). <u>Qualitative reading inventory.</u>
Illinois: Scott, Foresman and Company.

Manzo, A.V., Manzo, U.C. & McKenna, M.C. (1995) <u>Informal reading-thinking inventory.</u> Toronto: Harcourt Brace College Publishers.

Silveroli, N.J. (1994). <u>Classroom reading inventory.</u>
Iowa: Brown & Benchmark Publishers.

Steiglitz, E.L. (1992). <u>The Steiglitz informal reading inventory.</u>
Toronto: Allyn and Bacon.

Inside Back cover – prints blank